Mythical Mastery: Uncovering the Secrets of Legendary Beasts

Myrddin Sage

Published by Myrddin Sage, 2024.

MYTHICAL MASTERY: UNCOVERING THE SECRETS OF LEGENDARY BEASTS

First edition. December 16, 2024.

ISBN: 979-8230951681

Written by Myrddin Sage.

Table of Contents

Dedication

To the seekers of myths and the masters of imagination,

This book is dedicated to those who revel in the legends of old and dare to craft new tales of wonder. May your journey through the realms of mythology ignite your creativity and inspire you to weave your own stories of mythical mastery. Here's to the boundless power of imagination and the timeless allure of myths.

Mythical Mastery: Uncovering the Secrets of Legendary Beasts

Transform Your Understanding of Mythology in Weeks—No More Confusion, Just Captivating Stories and Facts.

Preface

"The truth about stories is that that's all we are." — Thomas King.

In this exploration of legendary beasts, we delve into the rich tapestry of mythology that has painted the imaginations of humanity across time and space. From the fire-breathing dragons of Europe to the benevolent unicorns of Asia, every creature tells a story, and every story carries a fragment of truth about the cultures that dreamt them into existence.

My purpose in writing this book was fueled by a simple yet profound frustration I observed among peers and students alike—the scattered resources and the dense academic jargon that often cloaks the beautiful simplicity of mythological tales. This book aims to untangle those knots. It's designed to transform your understanding of these legendary creatures over the course of just a few weeks, replacing confusion with clarity and curiosity with knowledge.

I remember vividly, during a lecture on cultural symbolism, a student—let's call her Sarah—expressed her dismay at how challenging it was to find accessible yet comprehensive materials on mythical creatures. She wasn't alone. Many shared her plight, struggling to connect deeply with the subject due to the lack of engaging content that could also educate. Stories like Sarah's planted the seeds for this book. If you've ever felt lost in the labyrinth of mythological studies, this is your guide out.

The inspiration for this journey came from academic circles and countless conversations with artists and writers who sought to incorporate these mythical elements into their work with authenticity and respect. Their passion for accurate representation and the sheer beauty of these myths propelled me forward.

A heartfelt thank you to all who contributed to this book. Their extensive knowledge of folklore provided a foundational pillar for my research. My gratitude extends to each interviewee, contributor, and peer reviewer, whose insights have enriched this work immeasurably.

To those who have picked up this book, thank you for inviting these stories into your life. Your curiosity and enthusiasm make endeavors like this worthwhile. I hope to not only fill knowledge gaps but also ignite a passion for the myths that have shaped human history and consciousness.

This book is crafted for mythology enthusiasts, artists, students of cultural studies, and anyone who finds joy in unraveling past mysteries as portrayed through mythical narratives. No prior expertise is required—just an open mind and a keen interest in the lore of ages.

As we turn these pages together, we embark on a journey through the lore of fantastical beasts and the very essence of human culture and imagination. ***Dive deep*** into these pages and emerge with treasures of knowledge that connect you more profoundly to our world's shared myths.

Thank you for beginning this adventure. Continue reading, and together, let's uncover the secrets of legendary beasts that have captivated hearts and minds through the millennia.

Chapter 1: Dragons Across Cultures: Symbols of Fear or Reverence?

Can Wisdom and Malevolence Coexist in the Realm of Dragons?

In the dim light of a quiet study, James pored over ancient texts that whispered secrets of dragons from different corners of the world. His fingers traced the delicate outlines of illustrations, each dragon curling across the page like a wave—some menacing with bared fangs, others serene with wise eyes. The room smelled of old paper and pine wood, a scent that usually comforted him but only deepened his restlessness today.

Outside, the wind stirred the autumn leaves into a dance, mirroring the turmoil in James's mind. He had always believed in the inherent good of mythical creatures, shaped by his grandmother's tales where dragons symbolized wisdom and protection. Yet here he was, confronted by starkly different depictions that depicted them as creatures to be feared in Western lore. This clash troubled him deeply as he prepared for tomorrow's lecture at the university—a lecture he hoped would bridge cultural myths with modern values.

His wife Maria entered quietly, her presence like a calm after a storm. She noticed his furrowed brow and touched his shoulder gently. *"Still wrestling with your dragons?"* she asked softly.

James smiled wryly. *"Trying to understand how something can represent both good and evil so distinctly depending on where you are in the world."* He gestured towards the papers scattered around him. *"It's fascinating yet frustrating."*

Maria picked up an ancient-looking scroll depicting an Eastern dragon amidst clouds. *"Maybe it's not about them being one or the other but showing us that everything has two sides."* Her voice was thoughtful as she replaced the scroll carefully on its pile.

The room fell silent again except for the crackling fire that cast flickering shadows over James's features. He pondered Maria's words, considering how this duality could be woven into his lecture to provoke thought rather than provide answers.

As night deepened around them and an owl hooted softly outside, James finally stood up and stretched his tired muscles. Tomorrow would be another day filled with young minds eager to explore these ancient myths through new lenses.

Could understanding these dualities within mythical creatures help us better navigate our own complexities?

Unveiling the Dragon: From Menace to Protector

The dragon, a creature as enigmatic as it is powerful, has captivated human imagination across millennia and continents. Yet, despite its universal recognition, the dragon embodies a spectrum of meanings that vary dramatically from one culture to another. This duality enriches its mythical stature and offers a unique lens through which we can explore deep-seated cultural values and beliefs globally. In this exploration of dragons across diverse traditions, we begin to unravel how these legendary beasts are not just creatures of fantasy but pivotal cultural symbols that reflect human psychology's and society's complexities.

At the heart of this investigation is a compelling contrast: ***in Western cultures***, dragons often emerge as formidable adversaries, embodiments of chaos and evil that heroes must conquer.

Conversely, ***in Eastern traditions,*** they frequently assume roles of guardianship and wisdom, revered as benevolent forces that bring prosperity and order. This stark contrast is not merely a matter of artistic interpretation but a reflection of the philosophical and moral frameworks that underpin different societies.

Cultural Reflections through Mythical Lenses

The symbolic significance attached to dragons extends beyond their roles in folklore; it taps into fundamental aspects of human belief and value systems. For instance, the Western perception of dragons as malevolent could be tied to Judeo-Christian narratives where serpentine figures often symbolize sin and moral downfall.

Meanwhile, in many Asian cultures, the dragon's divine attributes align with ideals of harmony and spiritual insight, mirroring philosophies such as Taoism and Buddhism that emphasize balance and enlightenment.

A Global Tapestry of Tales

In examining these mythical creatures, we also delve into how dragons have been depicted in various art forms—from ancient scrolls to modern cinema—and how these representations have evolved alongside changes in cultural attitudes. This artistic exploration is about aesthetic appreciation and understanding how mythology adapts to contemporary values and technologies.

The Power of Myth in Modern Identity

Furthermore, by studying these legendary dragons, we touch upon how myths help shape national identities and personal ideologies. Myths are not static relics of the past but dynamic narratives that continue to influence contemporary culture and politics. Understanding the dragon's role in these narratives can provide insights into global issues such as cultural conflict and integration.

Mastering Mythology

Embarking on this journey through mythical landscapes promises more than just academic knowledge; it offers a transformational perspective on how we view history, culture, and perhaps most importantly—ourselves. By mastering these myths, readers can expect to gain a deeper understanding of legendary beasts and an enhanced appreciation for the storytelling craft that has shaped human civilization.

As we navigate through this chapter and beyond, our aim is not just to inform but to inspire—a call to see beyond dragons' scales and wings to the core themes they embody about humanity itself.

Through thoughtful exploration and reflective inquiry, we uncover secrets about mythical creatures and timeless truths about human nature.

This discourse on dragons sets the stage for broader discussions on other mythical beings throughout this book. Each chapter builds on this foundation, weaving together tales of griffins, unicorns, and other fantastical entities into a rich tapestry that spans cultures and epochs—ultimately offering readers a comprehensive understanding of mythology free from confusion or superficiality.

Dragons have long captivated the human imagination, embodying both terror and wisdom across different cultures. In Western traditions, dragons often appear as fire-breathing beasts, symbols of chaos and destruction. They are the adversaries of heroes in many myths, exemplifying ultimate challenges to be overcome. In contrast, Eastern cultures celebrate dragons as wise and benevolent creatures, often associated with prosperity, luck, and the natural elements, particularly water. This stark difference in portrayal reflects deep-rooted cultural perceptions and values.

Imagine a dragon as a river. In the East, this river is life-giving, nurturing crops and civilizations, revered and respected along its banks. In the West, the same river might be seen during a flood, destructive and uncontrollable, something to be tamed or defeated.

This analogy helps to underline how the same creature can represent vastly different concepts based on cultural context.

The role of dragons in folklore and mythology can thus be seen as a mirror, reflecting how societies view the unknown and the supernatural. Western narratives often position dragons as obstacles in the path of human heroes—gatekeepers that protagonists must defeat to achieve their goals or save their communities. This portrayal can be linked to a broader narrative of man versus nature, a typical Western philosophy and literature theme.

In Eastern mythology, dragons often hold a more integral, positive role within the cosmic order. They are respected, celebrated with festivals, and depicted in art as symbols of power and wisdom.

Their association with weather and water elements showcases their importance in agriculture-based societies, where controlling them means survival and prosperity.

The dichotomy in dragon symbolism between East and West highlights the influence of cultural values on mythological storytelling. While the West often emphasizes the hero's journey against chaos, the East might focus on harmony and balance with the natural world.

Dragons are powerful symbols that reflect contrasting cultural values: feared destroyers in some traditions and revered guardians in others.

Exploring Symbolic Meanings

Dragons carry a variety of meanings within different cultural contexts, each adding layers to their mythological significance. In many Western stories, dragons are guardians of treasures, not just physically but metaphorically, guarding profound fears and great wisdom that require courage to confront. This can be seen as a metaphor for personal trials and the journey to overcome their deepest fears.

Conversely, in Eastern traditions, dragons often symbolize elements of nature, particularly water. They are seen as bringers of rain, essential for the prosperity of crops and, consequently, the prosperity of the people. Here, dragons are not obstacles but allies critical to human life, intertwined with the survival and flourishing of entire civilizations.

The symbolic role of dragons extends beyond mere character portrayal; it encapsulates fundamental aspects of human psychology and societal values. The dragon's dual representation as both fiend and friend invites us to consider how our cultural surroundings shape our perceptions.

The power of a dragon in a story can serve as a bridge between the natural world and the supernatural. In some cultures, dragons embody chaos and untamed nature, while in others, they harmonize the world's elements, crucial to maintaining balance in the universe.

Consider how dragons' symbolic meanings might reflect broader themes in human culture, such as the struggle between chaos and order or the importance of harmony with nature. Dragons' narrative significance is a profound commentary on human values and societal organization.

What might it reveal about our own cultural biases and perceptions if we delve deeper into these symbolic meanings?

Cultural Values and Beliefs Shape Dragon Narratives

The narratives surrounding dragons are deeply embedded in the cultural soil from which they spring. Western tales often highlight a fear of the unknown, portraying dragons as challenges to be overcome, much like the rugged, individualistic heroes common in Western folklore. This narrative reinforces values of bravery, conquest, and triumph over adversity.

In many Eastern tales, dragons are integral to the cosmology and spiritual life of the community. They are often seen as ancestors or gods, embodying wisdom and authority. This portrayal reflects values of respect for tradition and harmony with the natural world, which are pivotal in many Eastern societies.

The way dragons are woven into cultural narratives can reflect a culture's deepest values and beliefs. It's as if each society holds up a mirror to its collective psyche through the stories it tells of these mythical creatures. These stories are not just entertainment; they are a way of encoding and transmitting a culture's philosophic, ethical, and spiritual underpinnings.

Dragons, therefore, are more than mythical creatures; they are cultural symbols, each version shaped by humans' need to express aspects of their world and their place within it. The narratives surrounding them are shaped by a society's collective hopes, fears, and values.

The portrayal of dragons across different cultures highlights the diversity of human mythology and underscores the deep cultural values and beliefs that influence these narratives, reflecting a complex tapestry of human thought and civilization.

Dragons have captivated the human imagination across continents and cultures, embodying a range of emotions from awe to fear.

This chapter delves into the fascinating dichotomy of dragons in Western and Eastern cultures. It reveals how these mythical creatures are more than just fantastical beasts; they are profound symbols reflecting deep cultural values and beliefs.

Step 1: Differentiating Western and Eastern portrayals of dragons

We began by exploring the stark contrasts in dragon depictions between Western and Eastern traditions. In Western narratives, dragons often appear as menacing creatures with formidable wings and the ability to breathe fire, symbolizing chaos and destruction.

Conversely, with their serpentine forms and benevolent wisdom, Eastern dragons represent prosperity and protection. These visual and symbolic differences are not merely artistic choices but are deeply rooted in historical and cultural contexts that reflect each society's values.

Step 2: Exploring the symbolic meanings attached to dragons

Our journey continued with an exploration of the rich symbolism associated with dragons. Whether as omens of doom or bearers of wisdom, dragons occupy a significant place in mythology. By examining legends like that of the Chinese dragon, revered for its divine authority and association with natural elements, and contrasting it with the European dragon, often slain by heroes in epic battles, we gain insights into how societies project their ideals and fears onto these mythical beings.

Step 3: Discussing the cultural values and beliefs that shape dragon narratives

Finally, we delved into how dragons reflect societies' evolving values and beliefs. From ancient symbols of nature's untamed force to modern depictions in film and literature, where dragons symbolize complex characters capable of both good and evil, the narrative of the dragon is continually reshaped by cultural currents.

This evolution invites us to reflect on our own views and the mythological frameworks we inherit and adapt in our storytelling.

As we transition from this exploration of dragons to the broader realms of mythical creatures in the following chapters, remember that each beast carries a world of meaning waiting to be uncovered.

Armed with a deeper understanding of these symbols, you are better equipped to peel back the layers of narrative and symbolism that these creatures encapsulate.

Through this process, we appreciate the rich tapestry of global mythology and understand how deeply intertwined these stories are with human culture and psychology. Each step in this journey enlightens and empowers us to see beyond the myths themselves—to the very heart of human nature and our collective history.

Let this be a stepping stone into a world where myths are not just tales of old but keys to understanding deep cultural truths. As we venture further into the realms of mythical mastery, the secrets of legendary beasts await to transform our understanding of mythology and ourselves.

Chapter 2: Griffins in Antiquity: More than Mythical?

When Myth Meets Reality: The Curious Case of the Griffin

In the quiet corner of a dimly lit study, Professor Elara Jennings sat surrounded by mountains of ancient texts and scrolls, her eyes flickering with the reflection of the candlelight as she pored over an ancient manuscript. The walls, lined with shelves brimming with dusty books, seemed to lean in closer, listening to the soft rustle of pages turning. The air was thick with the scent of aged paper and wax.

Elara's mind was far away in ancient Scythia, where griffins guarded treasures beyond human reach. Her heart raced as she imagined these majestic creatures—part lion, part eagle—so vivid in their description that they seemed to leap off the parchment. She had stumbled upon a series of texts that described griffins and claimed their existence as guardians of gold. The thought fascinated her: what if these mythical beasts were more than symbols? What if they actually roamed the earth once?

She leaned back in her chair, her fingers tapping against the wooden desk. The candlelight cast shadows that danced across her face, mirroring the turmoil within her—a blend of excitement and skepticism. A cool breeze wafted through the open window, carrying the distant sounds of the city at night. Elara shivered slightly but was too engrossed to rise and close it.

Across her desk lay an open notebook filled with sketches she had drawn based on descriptions from various cultures: griffins as protectors, symbols of divine power, and creatures bridging earthly and heavenly realms. Each drawing reflected a folklore tied deeply to human belief and fear.

Could these myths be rooted in some forgotten truth? Elara wondered if these creatures had existed in some form—misinterpretations by early explorers seeing fossils or unknown animals for the first time. She imagined leading an expedition to unearth evidence that could turn myth into reality.

The clock struck midnight; its chime echoed through the room like a reminder from time itself not to get lost in fantasies too deep. Yet, how could one not dream when every historical account read like an invitation to explore worlds unseen?

Elara felt herself at a crossroads between history and mythology as she prepared for another long night delving into civilizations long gone but preserved through stories told from generation to generation. Was she merely chasing shadows cast by ancient firesides, or was there indeed something monumental waiting to be discovered about these legendary guardians?

How much do our beliefs shape what we perceive as reality?

Did Griffins Ever Roam the Earth?

Imagine a creature with a lion's body and an eagle's wings. Sounds like something out of a fantasy novel. Yet, in ancient times, the griffin was not just a mythical beast but a believed reality. This chapter delves into the fascinating perception of griffins as real entities. It explores their profound impact on various ancient cultures.

Griffins captivate our imagination and challenge our understanding of the past. Historically, these creatures were more than just symbols; they were part of many ancient societies' lived experiences and belief systems. ***The historical belief in griffins*** as real creatures highlights an intriguing intersection between mythology and perceived reality. People didn't just fear or revere these creatures; they integrated them into their daily lives, art, and economies.

The symbolic significance of combining a lion and an eagle into one majestic creature speaks volumes about the values and aspirations of ancient civilizations. Lions are often considered the kings of beasts, and eagles, seen as sovereigns of the sky, symbolize power, authority, and dominance. The griffin thus emerges not only as a creature of might but also as an emblem of ultimate control and protection. This amalgamation was no casual choice but a deliberate depiction to convey a powerful message.

Moreover, examining ***how the griffin's image influenced ancient societies*** offers insight into how myths shape cultural norms and worldviews. Griffins adorned palace walls, were woven into tapestries, and even influenced military strategies with their embodiments of strength and vigilance. Their presence in art and culture was both inspirational and instructional.

Throughout this exploration, we'll uncover how these legendary beasts weren't merely figments of imagination but integral to cultural identity and understanding in antiquity. By studying griffins, we tap into the broader narrative of human interaction with myth and nature's elements.

Reflecting on these aspects encourages us to reconsider what we classify as 'myths' and recognize the profound truths that myths communicate about human hopes, fears, and aspirations. As we navigate this chapter, let us keep an open mind about what constitutes reality and how legends can sometimes reveal deeper truths than historical facts alone.

This journey into the world of griffins is more than an academic inquiry—it's a voyage back to our ancestors' mindscape, where the fantastic and the factual blended seamlessly. Let's embark on this path with curiosity and wonder as our guides.

Understanding Historical Beliefs

Historically, griffins were not just creatures of myth; they were believed to be as real as any other animal spotted in the wild. This belief was prevalent in several ancient civilizations, including the Greeks and

Persians. Artifacts such as pottery and sculptures depict griffins as vividly as they do lions and eagles, suggesting that people of the time regarded them as part of the natural world.

Imagine that you are an ancient traveler traversing vast and unknown lands. Coming across a creature with a lion's body and an eagle's wings, you would likely believe it to be as natural as any other marvel you'd seen on your journeys. This analogy helps to understand how the ancients might have perceived such a magnificent beast.

Many ancient texts mention griffins in the same breath as real animals. The Greek historian Herodotus wrote about *"griffins guarding gold"* in the far north, where no man dared to venture. This insertion into everyday lore and geography marks the griffin not as a fanciful creature but as a part of the world's fauna to the people of that time.

The belief in griffins speaks volumes about ancient societies' knowledge and understanding of the natural world. It reflects a blend of observed reality and imaginative embellishment, which was common in the storytelling of that era. This blend allowed the griffin to soar in men's minds, not just as a symbol but as a living creature.

The historical belief in griffins underscores their reality in the minds of our ancestors, integrating them into the natural and mythological narratives of ancient cultures.

Symbolic Significance of the Griffin

The griffin combines the most majestic traits of the lion, the king of beasts, and the eagle, the king of birds. This amalgamation is not merely a fantastical zoological mix but a powerful symbolic gesture. It embodies the ultimate sovereign of the animal kingdom, both on land and in the sky.

In heraldry, the griffin is often used to denote strength, vigilance, and spiritual protection. These attributes are derived from the lion's courage and the eagle's keen sight. The use of the griffin in such a context suggests that it was seen as a guardian figure, capable of both great ferocity and majestic grace.

One could see the griffin as a bridge between two worlds—the earth and the sky. With its dual nature, this creature represents the aspiration to possess the qualities of the most wondrous land and air animals. It symbolizes a desire to transcend ordinary limitations, embodying the virtues of rulership, courage, and insight.

Combining these two kings of their respective realms, the griffin also serves as a metaphor for unity and power. It is as if the creature were designed to be the ultimate emblem of leadership and authority, revered for its might and vision.

The symbolism of the griffin teaches us about the values and aspirations of ancient societies, reflecting their ideals of courage, protection, and superiority.

Could understanding the griffin's symbolic blend of lion and eagle better illuminate the ancient world's view on power and protection?

The Griffin's Influence on Ancient Societies

The majestic image of the griffin had a profound influence on ancient societies. It was not merely a creature of wonder but a symbol of divine favor and protection. In cultures from Greece to Persia, griffins were depicted as guarding treasures and thrones, emphasizing their role as protectors of the sacred and the valuable.

Consider the griffin as a sentinel standing at the gates of a splendid city. Its presence conveys protection and a clear message of the city's grandeur and importance. This metaphor helps us understand how the image of the griffin could elevate the status of a place or a person in the eyes of the ancient world.

Griffins were often integrated into the artistic expressions of these societies, appearing on armor, pottery, and coins. This reinforced their symbolic importance and made their image a common sight that permeated many aspects of daily life.

The influence of the griffin's image was so pervasive that it transcended mere decoration. It became a part of the societal identity, embodying ideals of strength and vigilance crucial to these ancient peoples.

The griffin's portrayal in ancient art and lore illustrates its integral role in symbolizing divine protection and royal majesty, influencing everything from military regalia to architectural motifs.

By understanding the historical belief in their actual existence, analyzing their symbolic significance, and examining their influence on society, we gain a comprehensive view of the griffin's role in ancient mythology and its lasting legacy in cultural history.

Reflecting on the historical belief in griffins, it is fascinating to consider how ancient societies were not merely indulging in fantastical thinking but were earnestly engaging with what they perceived as a tangible part of their natural world. The griffin, composed of the lion and the eagle, symbolized a profound mix of majesty and power that resonated deeply within these cultures. The idea that such a beast could roam the earth speaks volumes about the values and fears of those times.

Griffins were more than mythical creatures; they were emblematic of the virtues and dangers that ancient people sought to understand and embody. By analyzing the symbolic significance of the griffin, we uncover layers of meaning in the fusion of these two regal animals. The lion's strength and the eagle's sovereignty combined to create a powerful icon demanding respect and inspiring awe.

Moreover, the griffin's influence extended beyond mere symbolism. It shaped cultural narratives and artistic expressions, infusing societies with wonder and caution. The belief in their existence underscores how mythology and reality can intertwine, enriching our understanding of past civilizations and their worldviews.

This exploration into griffins broadens our knowledge of ancient myths. It enriches our understanding of how these legends reflect and shape human thought. As we move forward in this book, let us carry with us the awe-inspiring image of the griffin, a reminder of humanity's perennial quest to give meaning to the natural and supernatural alike.

Through thoughtful examination and reflective insights, we come to appreciate not just the stories themselves but also their enduring impact on human culture and consciousness. Let this journey into the realm of legendary beasts continue to inspire and enlighten us as we seek to unravel more secrets held within the annals of mythology.

Chapter 3: Unicorns: Bridging Eastern and Western Mythologies

The Whisper of the Eastern Wind

The morning sun spilled its golden warmth over the ancient city, painting the narrow streets with hues of amber and rose. In one such lane, nestled between towering walls of weathered stone, Mingyu walked with a pace that matched the slow rhythm of the waking market. Vendors greeted him with nods and smiles, their stalls brimming with vibrant silks and fragrant spices. Yet, his mind wandered far from these familiar sights and scents.

Having spent years in the West, studying under scholars who often discussed mythical creatures, Mingyu found himself captivated by the unicorn. Its purity and grace, so revered in Western tales, had left a lasting impression on him. His return to the East was not just a homecoming, but a longing to bridge the ancient Eastern traditions with the enchanting Western myths he had come to admire.

As he passed a stall adorned with intricate jade carvings, an old man beckoned him closer. *"You seem troubled by thoughts heavier than our mountains,"* the elder said, his voice as soft as falling cherry blossoms. Mingyu smiled faintly, surprised by this interruption yet comforted by its sincerity.

"I am indeed," Mingyu confessed. *"I am caught between worlds—the mystical beasts of the West and our own Eastern legends."* His fingers traced over a carving that resembled Qilin, an auspicious creature from local folklore often likened to unicorns but imbued with symbols of prosperity and peace unique to Asian culture.

The elder's eyes sparkled like stars in twilight. *"Ah, but isn't that a splendid place to be? Between worlds is where true magic breathes life into new ideas,"* he said, his words carrying the weight of wisdom.

Mingyu pondered this as they talked more about how myths serve as tales and cultural bridges—each unicorn or Qilin carrying deeper meanings about human values and societal aspirations across continents.

As he left the elder behind, Mingyu felt lighter somehow—as if he understood that his struggle was not merely personal but part of a larger narrative weaving through time and space.

One could find universal truths about human nature in exploring these mythical beings from both worlds.

Discover the Magical Threads that Bind East and West Through the Myth of the Unicorn

Unicorns have long pranced through the pages of Western fairy tales, their ivory horns gleaming with promises of purity and grace.

Yet, these enigmatic creatures are not solely the treasures of Western lore; they also gallop through the vast landscapes of Eastern mythology, embodying a similar spectrum of virtues but viewed through a different cultural lens. This exploration into the mythical unicorn across diverse cultures reveals not just a fantastical animal but a symbol of universal ideals that resonate with all of us, shaped distinctly by regional beliefs.

At first glance, the unicorn might appear as merely a fanciful beast fit for children's books and medieval tapestries. However, a deeper dive into its story reveals complex layers of meaning that resonate across continents. In Western tradition, the unicorn is often seen as a wild woodland creature, elusive and pure, sometimes associated with chivalric quests and Christian symbolism. Contrastingly, in East Asian cultures, particularly in China and Japan, the unicorn takes on an entirely different persona—often more dragon-like in appearance and tied deeply to prosperity, peace, and political harmony.

The Cultural Significance of Unicorns

Understanding how unicorns are portrayed differently in Eastern and Western contexts allows us to see more than just mythical creatures;

it gives us profound insights into what different societies hold sacred. In Europe, the unicorn is frequently linked with purity and grace—a beacon of hope and an emblem of incorruptible power. However, across the seas in Asia, it symbolizes harmony and success, integral to blessings and good fortune. This comparative study enriches our understanding of cultural values and beliefs.

Symbols Across Cultures: Purity, Grace, and Power

As we delve into how unicorns represent these lofty concepts across various societies, we begin to uncover the deeper moral and spiritual lessons these myths convey. Why does purity manifest as a central theme both in tales of knights venerating unicorns in misty forests of Europe and in stories where Asian kings witness unicorn visitations as omens of wise rule? This chapter seeks to untangle these threads by comparing how these attributes align with broader cultural values.

Reflecting Prosperity and Peace Through Myth

Moreover, by evaluating how unicorns reflect prosperity and peace in Asian traditions compared to their Western counterparts, we gain insights into each culture's worldview. It's fascinating that Western narratives often focus on the individual's journey toward greatness or moral rectitude via encounters with unicorns. Eastern stories emphasize communal harmony and societal blessings that such encounters portend.

Through this exploration, readers are invited to traverse mythical realms and reflect on their cultural foundations—what virtues do we uphold? What symbols resonate within our own societies? How do our myths shape our understanding of virtue and vice?

We uncover a shared human fascination with creatures that embody our highest ideals by bridging these mythical narratives from East to West. This chapter promises to be an enlightening journey through time-honored tales where myth meets morality across cultures—a true testament to the power of legendary beasts to unite us under common human themes.

In summarizing this panoramic view, before delving deeper into specifics throughout this chapter, let us remember how understanding these symbolic creatures can enrich our knowledge of mythology and our place within this intricately woven tapestry of human culture. The study of unicorns is not just a fascinating exploration, but a crucial aspect of understanding the human psyche and our cultural heritage.

Unicorns Across Cultures

For instance, in Western lore, unicorns are often depicted as majestic, pure white horses with a single spiraling horn, symbolizing purity and grace. In contrast, Eastern traditions portray unicorns differently, sometimes resembling a deer or dragon, and are associated with prosperity and peace, as seen in the Chinese Qilin.

For example, in the West, the unicorn's appearance as a pure white horse with a single horn symbolizes its role as a guardian of the forest and its connection to the divine. On the other hand, the eastern unicorn, like the Chinese Qilin, with its scaly body and ethereal presence, represents prosperity and peace, reflecting the cultural values of communal harmony and societal blessings.

This contrast in appearance and symbolism between the East and West opens a fascinating dialogue about cultural values. In the West, the unicorn is often seen as a guardian of the forest, a rare and untouchable creature that embodies purity and grace. Its counterpart in the East takes a more communal role, often seen interacting with people, guiding them towards wisdom and justice, and symbolizing prosperity and peace.

Imagine a garden where every flower represents a different culture's take on mythical creatures. The Western unicorn might be a white rose, pure and beautifully simple. The Eastern unicorn, however, could be a vibrant chrysanthemum, complex and integral to the community's fabric.

Unicorns serve distinct roles in Eastern and Western mythologies, reflecting the diverse tapestries of cultural values and beliefs.

The Essence of Unicorns: Purity, Grace, and Power

Unicorns are universally admired for their inherent qualities of purity, grace, and power. However, these attributes are interpreted and valued differently across cultures. In Western myths, the unicorn's purity is often linked with virginity and innocence, symbolizing divine love and spiritual truth.

The grace of a unicorn is not just in its appearance but also in its movement and interaction with the world. It moves through the forest with such elegance that not a single blade of grass bends unnecessarily under its weight.

In terms of power, unicorns are physically formidable and magically potent. They can heal wounds and purify water, a testament to their strength and benevolence. This power, however, is wielded with a humility that only heightens their grace.

Considering their power and grace, imagine unicorns as both the storm and the calm within it. Their strength is as formidable as a tempest, yet they also bring peace, like the stillness after a storm.

How do these interpretations of purity, grace, and power influence our understanding of virtue and strength in our own lives?

Reflecting Cultural Values Through Mythical Unicorns

The perception of unicorns goes beyond their mystical attributes; it reflects underlying cultural values of prosperity and peace, particularly evident in Eastern mythology. The Qilin, for instance, is seen not only as a creature of good fortune but also as a guardian of principles.

In many Asian cultures, the unicorn's role in bringing prosperity is tied to its moral rectitude. It appears during the reign of benevolent rulers or in times of peace. Its presence is both a reflection of and a catalyst for societal harmony and prosperity.

This connection between mythical creatures and cultural values can be likened to a mirror reflecting a society's priorities and aspirations. Just as a mirror shows us our external appearance, mythology's unicorns reflect a culture's internal moral and ethical compass.

By understanding the roles and symbolism of unicorns in various cultures and how they embody purity, grace, and power, we can see how these creatures mirror the values of prosperity and peace across different societies, thus bridging Eastern and Western mythologies in a shared narrative of mythical significance.

Unicorns: A Universal Symbol

Unicorns have long captured our imaginations, appearing in both Eastern and Western mythologies as symbols of purity, grace, and power. This chapter has taken us through these cultural landscapes, revealing how these mythical creatures are perceived and revered worldwide. Their symbolism transcends geographical boundaries, reflecting a shared human fascination with the magical and the pure.

Unicorns in Different Cultures

Our exploration began by comparing the roles unicorns play across different societies. In Western traditions, the unicorn is often seen as a wild woodland creature, elusive and beautiful, symbolizing purity and grace. On the other hand, in East Asian cultures, similar mythical creatures like the Qilin bring forth associations of prosperity and peace, marking significant cultural values prioritizing communal harmony and success.

Symbolism of Purity and Grace

We delved into how unicorns represent physical purity and the power of grace. Despite their mythical status, these creatures encourage us to pursue the purest forms of ourselves. They remind us of the strength in gentleness and the power of being true to one's moral compass.

Reflections of Cultural Values

The perception of unicorns as symbols of prosperity and peace in Eastern mythologies contrasts with their Western counterparts, providing a fascinating lens through which we can view cultural values. This difference underscores the broader theme of how societies use myths to encapsulate and communicate cherished ideals and aspirations.

Through this chapter, we've seen that unicorns' allure lies not only in their mystical attributes but also in what they stand for across cultures. They are more than mythical beasts; they are bearers of hope, purity, and the endless possibilities that come with peace.

By understanding these magnificent creatures' roles in various cultures, we gain insights into mythology and the human condition. Our journey through the myths of unicorns encourages us to reflect on our values and the myths we hold dear in our own lives.

As we continue to explore other legendary beasts in this book, let us remember the lessons learned from unicorns. Let their symbolism inspire us to seek out the magical in the mundane and strive for a world characterized by purity, grace, and peace.

Chapter 4: Art and Text: Portals to Mythical Realities

Can Ancient Myths Unveil Truths in Modern Times?

In the dusky light of early evening, Thomas ambled through the crowded streets of Athens, his mind a tangled weave of ancient myth and modern reality. He was a scholar, but today, he felt more like an explorer, seeking truths that seemed lost in time. The city buzzed around him with the life of the present, yet he could not shake off the whispers of its storied past.

He paused before a replica of an ancient Greek sculpture displayed outside the National Archaeological Museum. The figure was that of Chimera, a mythical creature with the head and body of a lion, a goat's head protruding from its back, and a serpent for a tail. In popular films and books back home, Chimera was often depicted as merely a monstrous beast to be slain by heroes. But here, under the shadowed gaze of history itself, Thomas knew there was more to understand—about Chimera, about myths themselves.

His thoughts drifted to an earlier conversation with Professor Alekos, who had passionately argued that returning to these original artworks could bridge the gap between ancient symbolism and contemporary interpretation. *"They are not just creatures,"* Alekos had said as they stood amidst age-old relics; *"they are symbols of natural phenomena, human fears, and societal challenges."*

As Thomas touched the cool marble of Chimera's replica, he connected to ancient artists who sought to encapsulate such complex meanings into their work. It was not just about capturing form but also essence. How far had modern interpretations strayed from what these creatures were meant to represent?

A child's laugh broke his reverie—a young boy tugging at his mother's hand pointed excitedly at Chimera. *"Look, Mommy! It's just like in my video game!"* he exclaimed before they disappeared into the museum.

Thomas smiled slightly but felt a twinge in his heart. Was this what myths had been reduced to? Simple characters in stories and games without depth or context? He wondered if he could help others see beyond this surface-level engagement by re-engaging with traditional art forms and texts.

As night fell over Athens and lights flickered on across the sprawling cityscape below him from his vantage point on an old stone balcony overlooking part of the historic center, Thomas considered how much deeper our understanding might be if we viewed these myths through their original lens.

Could revisiting ancient myths through their classical representations help us navigate our modern complexities?

Peeling Back the Layers of Myth: A Journey to Authenticity

In an age dominated by blockbuster films and fantasy novels, the true essence of mythical creatures often becomes clouded, their original meanings diluted in a sea of modern reinterpretations. It is crucial, therefore, to return to the foundational sources—classical art and ancient texts—to recapture the authentic spirit and profound symbolism these beings once held. This chapter delves into why and how revisiting these original depictions can transform our understanding of mythical lore.

The Vital Role of Original Sources

Original texts and artworks serve as direct portals into the minds and cultures of our ancestors, offering unfiltered insights into their worldviews. By engaging with these sources, we gain historical knowledge and develop a deeper connection with the past. The significance of this approach lies in its ability to provide a more nuanced understanding of mythical creatures beyond the surface-level portrayals commonly seen today.

Classical Art and Literature: Windows to Ancient Wisdom

Classical sculptures, paintings, and literary works are more than mere artifacts; they are rich with context and meaning. Analyzing these elements allows us to see how ancient civilizations perceived and valued mythical creatures within their cultural fabric. Such an exploration reveals the layers of symbolism that modern interpretations often overlook or misunderstand.

Correcting Modern Misconceptions

One of the most compelling reasons to study ancient representations is to correct contemporary misconceptions. Today's media frequently reshapes mythical figures to fit modern narratives, sometimes straying far from their original significance.

By grounding our understanding in historical accuracy, we can appreciate the aesthetic and ideological impacts of these creatures.

The journey through classical art and literature is not just an academic exercise but a path toward reclaiming a more authentic, enriched view of mythology that resonates with historical truths rather than commercialized fiction. This deeper appreciation creates new dimensions in understanding human culture and creativity across ages.

Our exploration will not merely skim the surface but will dive deep into specific examples, highlighting how traditional depictions can enlighten current perspectives. This method upholds the enjoyment of contemporary interpretations but enhances it by adding layers of meaning and context.

By reconnecting with the roots of these legendary beasts through careful study and reflection, we stand to gain not just knowledge but wisdom—a wisdom that teaches us about the complexities of human imagination and belief systems throughout history. This chapter promises to be both a retrospective journey and a reawakening to the wonders of mythology, as seen through the eyes of those who first envisioned such magnificent creatures.

Exploring the Importance of Original Sources

Imagine you are a detective in a vast library, and your mission is to uncover the true essence of mythical creatures. Each scroll and sculpture is a clue, and each ancient text is a coded message. By returning to these original sources, we unveil the authentic narratives that have been woven into the fabric of ancient societies.

These artifacts are not just relics; they are the keys to understanding the profound symbolism that mythical creatures hold in their respective cultures.

In an era dominated by cinematic adaptations and reinterpretations, the original meanings of creatures like dragons, griffins, and phoenixes can become obscured. For instance, while modern portrayals often depict dragons as mere beasts for heroes to conquer, ancient texts like the ***Epic of Gilgamesh*** or Chinese mythology present them as complex symbols of chaos, wisdom, or guardianship. This disparity highlights the necessity of engaging with original sources to grasp these creatures' multifaceted roles.

Another layer to consider is the influence of translation and cultural interpretation over time. What was once a sacred emblem in one culture might be reduced to a generic villain in another. By delving into the original texts and art, we re-contextualize these beings within their historical and cultural backdrop, allowing for a richer, more accurate appreciation.

Artifacts like the Ishtar Gate of Babylon, adorned with dragons and lions, serve not just as decoration but as a testament to the reverence and fear these creatures inspired. Similarly, the intricate carvings of the Norse woodlands in the Viking era tell stories of mystical beings believed to influence life and death.

Returning to original sources is crucial for a proper understanding of mythical creatures.

Analyzing Classical Art and Literature

When we examine classical art and literature, we are not merely observing. We are engaging with the minds of ancient artists and writers, decoding symbols that have transcended time. Take, for example, the Greek pottery adorned with images of centaurs. These are not just decorative; they are narrative devices that convey intertwined stories of chaos, nature, and humanity.

Literary works such as Homer's ***Iliad*** and ***Odyssey*** are rich with depictions of mythical beings, each character playing a pivotal role that often reflects human virtues and vices. These texts use mythical creatures to embellish the narrative and explore deep philosophical questions about fate, power, and morality.

Rhetorical devices in these texts—like allegory and metaphor—enhance our understanding of how ancients viewed the cosmos and their place within it. A simple creature like the sphinx becomes a gatekeeper of knowledge, challenging heroes with riddles that probe their intellect and morality.

Visually, the frescoes of ancient Thera or the statues of Hindu gods are not just art; they embody divine and mortal interactions, capturing moments of mythological significance that offer insights into ancient people's fears, hopes, and values.

Could exploring these classical depictions be the key to unlocking a deeper connection with our past?

Framework for Analyzing Mythical Representations

An Analytical Framework for Decoding Mythical Beings

Identification

The first step in our framework involves identifying the mythical themes and symbols present in art and literature. This means recognizing a creature like a Griffin and understanding its implications—protector of divine power, a bridge between earth and sky. This stage is crucial as it sets the groundwork for deeper analysis.

Contextualization

Next, we place these elements within their historical, cultural, and geographical context. A Griffin depicted in Greek art might symbolize divine protection, while Persian art could represent royal power. Understanding the context allows us to see how the portrayal of mythical creatures varies with cultural beliefs and historical periods.

Interpretation

Finally, the interpretation stage involves deriving meaning from these contexts. We explore how these portrayals reflect societal values and human experiences. For instance, analyzing why certain creatures appear repeatedly in religious contexts might reveal their role in explaining natural phenomena or human psychology.

This framework deepens our understanding of ancient cultures and enriches our modern interpretation of these myths. By applying this model to specific examples, such as a Griffin on ancient pottery, we can demonstrate the practical application of these steps.

This framework ties together the need to return to original sources, analyze classical depictions, and assess their cultural significance, providing a comprehensive understanding of mythical creatures.

Journey Through the Mythical Lens

Embarking on a journey through the annals of mythology requires more than just a cursory glance at modern renditions; it necessitates a deep dive into the original sources that have chronicled these tales through the ages. The essence of understanding mythical creatures lies in revisiting the ancient texts and artworks that first brought them to life. This approach is not merely academic—it's a way to experience the rich tapestry of meanings and symbols as they were originally intended.

Step 1: Importance of Returning to Original Sources

Studying original sources like ancient sculptures, texts, and paintings is paramount. These materials serve as the most authentic glimpse into the past, offering insights that are often diluted or reinterpreted in modern adaptations. By engaging with these primary sources, we honor the integrity of these myths and gain a nuanced understanding that is otherwise lost. I encourage you to explore epic poems and classical art—not as historical curiosities but as living narratives that still resonate with profound truths about human nature and the universe.

Step 2: Analyzing Classical Art and Literature

Consider the power of a Greek vase painting or the verses of an epic poem. Each line and stroke holds a wealth of information about the time period, societal values, and, most importantly, the mythical beings depicted. When we analyze these pieces, we're not just uncovering facts; we're connecting with the minds of artists and poets who had their own interpretations of these myths. This step isn't just about observation; it's about interaction. Engage with these artworks and texts as if entering into a dialogue with history.

Step 3: Assessing Ancient and Traditional Representations

This step involves critically assessing how ancient representations shape our understanding of mythical creatures. It's about spotting the contrasts and continuities between past and present depictions. However, it's crucial to approach this task with both reverence and a critical eye, recognizing potential biases or cultural slants embedded in these portrayals. Reflect on how these ancient images and narratives influence your perception of mythology. What insights do they offer, and what limitations do they present?

By following these steps, you're not just learning about mythology; you're immersing yourself in a world where every artwork and text provides a portal to deeper understanding. This process is designed to transform your approach to mythical beings from one of passive reception to active engagement. Allow yourself approximately two weeks per step, giving ample time to absorb the details and reflect on their significance.

This journey through art and text is not just an academic exercise; it's a reconnection with our cultural heritage. As you delve into these ancient sources, you may find that these mythical creatures reveal as much about your own world as they do about their inhabited initial worlds.

Through this exploration, you contribute to your personal growth and the preservation of knowledge that might otherwise be lost to time's relentless march. Embrace this quest with curiosity and respect, and let each discovery inspire you to unravel the intricate web of mythology further.

Chapter 5: The Creative Spark: Mythology and Human Invention

Can Myths Forge the Future?

Professor Elena Mirov spent her evenings surrounded by the whispers of ancient civilizations in a small, cluttered study filled with ancient books and artifacts. The walls, lined with shelves burdened under the weight of history, seemed to lean in closer each night as if eager to share their secrets. The dim light from her desk lamp cast long shadows that danced across the room, mirroring the flickering doubts that often played across her mind.

Elena was not just a historian but a seeker of patterns, tracing the threads of human creativity through the tapestry of myths and legends. Tonight, like many before, she pondered over a particularly intriguing mythical beast—the Griffin. This creature, with a lion's body and an eagle's wings and head, symbolized strength and vigilance in ancient cultures. It was more than a figure of myth; it was a cultural bridge connecting diverse societies through shared themes of morality and philosophy.

As she turned the brittle pages of an old text detailing an archaeological dig near Thessaloniki where Griffin-like statuettes were unearthed, her cat, Apollo—named after the god of arts—jumped onto her desk. His sudden presence pulled her from thoughts. She smiled briefly at Apollo's interruption but quickly returned to her contemplation. How did these ancient symbols shape the ethical codes that guided civilizations? Were these creatures manifestations of collective human fears and aspirations?

Elena's mind drifted to her upcoming lecture on mythical symbolism in modern governance. Could understanding these ancient myths help today's leaders make better decisions? Myths were not mere stories but tools for teaching enduring lessons on leadership and morality.

Outside her window, the wind whispered through the leaves as if carrying secrets from ages past into our present world. Elena looked up from her book towards that sound—a gentle reminder that history was alive, constantly conversing with the present.

Could we learn from myths how to better shape our future?

Unveiling the Origins of Our Deepest Stories

When we delve into mythical beasts, we're not just exploring tall tales and fantastical creatures; we're peering into the essence of human creativity and cultural evolution. These creatures, born from the depths of human imagination, mirror our deepest fears, highest aspirations, and most profound values. This chapter will help you understand how these legendary beings are central figures in narratives and pivotal in shaping the tapestry of human thought across different epochs and societies.

The Artistry Behind Mythical Beasts

The creation of mythical beasts showcases an extraordinary aspect of human ingenuity. Every dragon's scale and each phoenix's feather weave together stories that have captivated audiences for centuries. Here, we explore how these beings are ***not mere figments*** but rather complex constructions that offer insights into the narrative skills of ancient cultures. We'll see how these creatures helped our ancestors make sense of the natural world around them, transforming fear into folklore.

Reflecting Cultures and Morals through Myths

Mythical creatures often carry with them the moral and ethical weight of the societies that created them. They act as carriers of cultural norms and are instrumental in passing these values across generations. This chapter delves into how stories about beasts like centaurs or griffins are imbued with lessons on morality and conduct, serving as both entertainment and ethical education for their audience.

The Universal Language of Myth-Making

Despite vast differences in geographical and cultural landscapes, myth-making has a striking universality. Whether it's the Nordic tales of trolls or the African stories about Anansi, mythical creatures serve similar roles worldwide: explaining the unexplainable and teaching the community's young ones about life's complex truths. This universality speaks to a shared human experience—a collective subconscious that spans across oceans and transcends time.

This chapter will enhance your appreciation for mythology and deepen your understanding of its role in human development by examining these themes. By tracing how these myths have morphed through time while retaining core narratives, we gain insight into the resilience and adaptability of human storytelling.

As we move forward, remember that each mythical beast carries with it more than just a story—it bears centuries of human thought, creativity, and wisdom. Let us tread lightly but curiously through this enchanted realm, where each creature teaches us not just about our past but also about our present and how we envision our future.

In our journey together through this chapter, prepare to unlock new ways of seeing myths and life itself. These stories are keys to unlocking universal truths about who we are as humans and how we interact with our world—truths that resonate just as powerfully today as they did when they were first told by firelight in ancient times.

Exploring the Illustration of Human Creativity through Mythical Creatures

Mythical creatures, from the fire-breathing dragons of European folklore to the shape-shifting kitsune of Japanese mythology, serve as a vibrant canvas showcasing the heights of human creativity. These beings are not merely products of whimsy but rather profound manifestations of the human capacity to invent and tell stories. Each creature's unique abilities and origin story reflect the diverse tapestry of human imagination across different cultures and eras.

Consider the analogy of a painter with a broad palette of colors. Just as a painter mixes colors to create new hues, storytellers blend personal experiences, cultural backgrounds, and human emotions to craft new mythical creatures. This process mirrors our creative spirit, highlighting our innate need to explore and understand the unknown through narrative.

The details embedded in these myths—such as the Hydra's regenerating heads or the cunning of Anansi the Spider—illustrate more than just fantastical elements. They underscore the storytellers' intricate understanding of human nature and desire to encapsulate complex moral and philosophical questions in engaging tales. Each story, each creature, serves as a conduit for conveying deeper truths about life, existence, and morality.

As these myths were told and retold, they evolved, much like oral traditions, adapting to the landscapes of their times. This evolution proves their role not just as stories but as living elements of human culture, continually reshaped by the collective human experience.

Revisiting and revising these myths is itself a creative endeavor, underscoring the dynamic nature of human creativity.

Mythical creatures exemplify the boundless creativity of human narrative invention.

Relating Mythical Beasts to Broader Cultural and Moral Themes

Mythical beasts often serve as metaphors for the values and ethics of the societies that created them. The majestic phoenix, for instance, symbolizes renewal and resilience in multiple cultures, from the ancient Egyptians to the Chinese. This common theme of rebirth highlights a universal human admiration for resilience and the ability to rise from adversity.

In exploring these creatures, we delve into a deeper understanding of human culture itself. The creatures often embody the moral codes of their times, acting as guardians of cultural mores or as warnings against moral transgression. For instance, the terrifying Greek Minotaur was a constant reminder of the consequences of unchecked power and the human sacrifices it can demand.

Rhetorical questions provoke deeper reflection here: What does our creation of such beasts say about us? Do these creatures reflect our deepest fears and highest hopes? By pondering these questions, one gains insight into ancient myths and the enduring human conditions they represent.

Studying these mythical creatures reveals patterns in human morality that transcend individual cultures. It showcases our collective need to express societal values and personal ethics through storytelling, a tradition as old as humanity itself. This myth-making tradition reflects a shared human endeavor to understand and convey the complexities of existence and coexistence.

Could understanding these mythical beasts be the key to understanding the very fabric of human moral philosophy?

Reflecting on Universal Storytelling and Myth-Making

The creation of myths is a universal human activity found in every corner of the world. This ubiquity suggests that myth-making is a cultural activity and a fundamental human impulse. Like the spider weaving its web, humans weave intricate stories to make sense of the world around them.

While diverse in form and function, these stories share common elements that suggest a shared human experience. Whether it's the hero's journey, the triumph over impossible odds, or the explanation of natural phenomena, these stories resonate with us because they reflect our own lives, struggles, and environments.

This reflection is not just about entertainment but about a deeper, almost instinctual need to communicate and preserve knowledge. Myths carry the essential truths and wisdom of a culture passed down through generations. The act of retelling these stories is a communal experience, reinforcing social bonds and shared values.

The global tapestry of myths, with its myriad threads, reveals the rich diversity yet fundamental similarities in how humans perceive and narrate their world. This realization fosters a deeper appreciation for both the uniqueness and the unity of human cultures.

By examining mythical creatures and the myths surrounding them, we gain insights into human creativity, cultural values, and universal storytelling, thus enriching our understanding of humanity across ages and civilizations.

Understanding the creations of mythology isn't just about exploring fantastical beasts and legendary creatures; it's about delving deep into the heart of human creativity and our enduring quest to make sense of the world around us. Through the lens of mythical beasts, we see not only the boundless realms of human imagination but also the profound ways these narratives are woven into the fabric of cultural and moral understanding across different societies.

Mythical creatures serve as mirrors, reflecting our deepest fears, greatest hopes, and most cherished values. These stories passed down through generations, do more than entertain—they educate, caution, and inspire. Studying these fantastical beings gives us insights into how our ancestors viewed the world and themselves.

This, in turn, offers us a unique perspective on our own times and perhaps a guidepost for the future.

It's fascinating to reflect on how these myths, despite arising from diverse cultures and epochs, share universal themes—good versus evil, chaos versus order, humility versus hubris. These recurring motifs underscore the shared human experience, highlighting that certain truths remain constant regardless of where or when we live.

Moreover, engaging with these stories encourages us to appreciate past artistic endeavors and continue the tradition of storytelling in our own lives. Each time we recount a myth or create a new narrative, we participate in a timeless ritual that binds us to each other and to those who came before us.

So, let this exploration of mythical creatures be more than an academic pursuit. Let it be a call to embrace our creative instincts, to tell new stories, and to keep alive the flame of imagination that has illuminated human existence for millennia. As we move forward in this book, remember that these tales are not just relics of the past but are vibrant threads in the ongoing tapestry of human culture. They challenge us to think, dream, and wonder—what new myths will we create together?

Chapter 6: Cultural Crossroads: Comparative Mythology

How Do Myths Shape Our Understanding of the World?

A brisk wind swept through the streets of a small town nestled at the edge of ancient mountains, tugging at the corners of faded posters and whispering secrets only old stones could comprehend. Usually a bustling hub, the market square lay quiet under the late afternoon sun. At one corner stood Marcus, an older man with eyes as deep as the lore he cherished. His gaze lingered on a group of children playing by an old fountain, their laughter mingling with the splash of water.

Marcus had spent his life studying comparative mythology, tracing the threads that wove together tales from different cultures. Today, however, his thoughts were not on his research but on his granddaughter, Mia. She was about to leave for university in a city far from their mountain shadows and folklore-filled evenings. The idea unsettled him; it was like watching an old tale lose its path in the woods.

He walked slowly towards his quaint bookshop, which smelled of musty pages and time. He pondered how stories shaped beliefs and values as he passed through aisles lined with ancient texts and newer analyses of mythological creatures across cultures. He remembered Mia's wide-eyed wonder when she first heard about dragons—not just the fierce beasts of Western tales but also the wise and benevolent dragons of Eastern myths.

Marcus paused by a window, watching dusk paint shadows on cobblestones. He thought about how dragons represented power and wisdom in some cultures while symbolizing destruction in others. It dawned on him that perhaps this was what he needed to share with

Mia—a lesson on perspective and understanding before she ventured into new terrains, both geographical and intellectual.

The bell above the door chimed as a breeze nudged it open slightly. Marcus turned back to his desk littered with notes for his next lecture: *"Cultural Intersections in Mythology."* A smile touched his lips as he imagined discussing it with Mia over their last dinner before her departure.

Could understanding these ancient myths help us navigate our modern world's cultural complexities?

Unveiling the Tapestry of Myths: A Journey Through Time and Culture

Mythology, with its intricate tapestry of stories and legends, mirrors the values, fears, and aspirations of cultures. As we delve into the realm of mythical beasts, we discover fantastical creatures and the profound intersections where different societies overlap, diverge, and influence one another. This exploration is not merely an academic exercise; it's a journey into the heart of human creativity and belief systems across various epochs and regions.

The Cultural Mosaic of Mythical Creatures

At first glance, mythical creatures might seem like mere figments of imagination—grist for fantastical tales. However, these beings often carry heavier burdens; they are vessels filled with cultural significance and historical context. Engaging with stories of dragons, phoenixes, or mermaids from different cultural backgrounds reveals a rich mosaic of human thought and societal values. It's fascinating to observe how a dragon holds a place of reverence in Chinese folklore, symbolizing power and good fortune, while in Western narratives, it often plays the role of a menacing antagonist.

Adaptation and Evolution in Mythological Narratives

Myths breathe life into the ethos of societies; they adapt over time to fit new eras and environments. This adaptive quality allows us to trace the paths through which cultures have interacted—whether through conquest, trade, or intellectual exchange. The evolution of vampire tales from ancient folklore to modern media is a prime example of this dynamic process. Initially rooted in regional superstitions about death and the afterlife, vampires have evolved into complex figures that challenge our understanding of morality and fear.

Myths as Catalysts for Cultural Exchange

The role of myths extends beyond mere storytelling; they act as catalysts for cultural exchange. Each retelling adds layers to the original narrative, colored by the lens of the current storyteller's cultural background. This process enriches both the story and its audience, offering insights into how different cultures handle universal themes like heroism, justice, and transformation.

By exploring these aspects—***the portrayal of mythical creatures across societies, the adaptation of myths over time***, and ***their role in cultural exchange***—we gain a deeper understanding of mythology and humanity itself. The stories might be ancient or modernized, but they still speak to fundamental human concerns: identity, conflict resolution, and the boundaries between good and evil.

Reflective Insights on Our Shared Histories

As we navigate these stories, we also embark on a reflective journey about our place within these narratives. What do our interpretations of these myths say about us today? How do they shape our view of the past and our hopes for the future? This reflective inquiry not only enhances our appreciation for mythology but also fosters a deeper connection with cultures around the world.

Thus begins our exploration into the labyrinthine world of myths across different landscapes—a journey that promises enlightenment about legendary beasts and ourselves. Through this comparative mythology study, we connect dots across time and space, constructing a more cohesive understanding of human civilization's vast narrative tapestry.

Herein lies an invitation to look beyond the surface—to explore how these legendary creatures reflect broader cultural dialogues that continue to shape our worldviews and artistic expressions. Join us on this enlightening journey to grasp how truly intertwined our stories are.

Engaging with Mythical Narratives

Mythical creatures often serve as mirrors, reflecting a society's values, fears, and aspirations. Dragons, for instance, appear in both European and Asian cultures, yet their roles and symbolism can vary dramatically. In Europe, dragons are typically powerful and malevolent entities to be conquered, as seen in the legend of Saint George. Conversely, in Chinese culture, dragons symbolize prosperity and are considered benevolent.

Imagine a tapestry, each thread representing a different story or myth worldwide. As we engage with these stories, we begin to see patterns—the intersections of these threads—revealing how societies influence each other culturally. This comparative approach helps us appreciate the uniqueness of each culture and their interconnectedness.

Observing how the same creature can embody different meanings in different cultures is fascinating. The serpent, often seen as a symbol of evil and trickery in Western narratives, is viewed as a protector and a symbol of rebirth in Hindu mythology. This divergence not only highlights cultural differences but also encourages a deeper exploration of each society's ethos.

Through the lens of mythology, we can trace the paths of cultural exchange and adaptation. The spread of myths across borders often transforms these stories, adapting to local values and norms. This ongoing evolution of myths offers dynamic insight into the fluid nature of human culture and storytelling.

By engaging with the diverse portrayals of mythical creatures across societies, we uncover the rich tapestry of cultural intersections.

Analyzing Mythical Adaptations

Mythical narratives are not static; they evolve as they are told and retold, influenced by various cultural exchanges. A prime example is the vampire legend, which has roots in Eastern European folklore but has been adapted globally, each version reflecting the societal concerns of its time.

Why do myths diverge in their journey across cultures? Consider a river that starts from a single source but branches off into myriad streams. Similarly, a myth begins in one culture, but as it spreads, it diverges, being influenced by the local cultural landscape and resulting in variations that may be starkly different from the original.

The adaptation of myths can be seen as a form of cultural dialogue, where stories are not merely borrowed but reshaped to fit the new cultural contexts. This reshaping can involve transforming characters, plotlines, and morals to better resonate with the new audience's values and experiences.

Rhetorical question: What does this adaptation process tell us about the societies that adopt and alter these myths? It reveals their priorities, challenges, and values in a way that factual historical records might not. Myths, in their adaptability, become a valuable tool for cultural analysis.

Analogies aside, studying these adaptations provides concrete insights into cultural interaction and assimilation mechanisms. By examining how myths change, we can gain insights into the broader processes of cultural change and continuity.

Could the way myths adapt and diverge in various cultural narratives be the key to understanding our society's values and fears?

The Role of Myths in Cultural Exchange

Myths are more than just entertainment; they are a fundamental part of the cultural exchange that shapes societies. The spread of myths across different regions often parallels historical routes of trade and conquest, illustrating how stories travel and transform along with people.

The role of myths in cultural exchange is akin to the role of a translator in a diplomatic meeting. Just as a translator interprets languages to foster understanding between delegates, myths translate core human experiences and values across cultural boundaries, promoting mutual understanding and respect.

This translation is only sometimes direct or literal. Myths adapt to their new environments, adopting local flavors while retaining their core narratives, much like a recipe that is tweaked to suit local tastes without losing its identity. This process enriches the receiving culture, offering new perspectives and ideas through the familiar structure of the myth.

Understanding these dynamics offers us a clearer picture of how cultures interact and evolve. By studying myths, we preserve these stories and facilitate an ongoing dialogue between past and present and between diverse cultures.

The exploration of myths across different cultures reveals their role in cultural exchange and historical adaptation, tying together our understanding of how societies learn, adapt, and influence each other through storytelling.

Unveiling the Tapestry of Myth

The journey through comparative mythology is akin to unraveling a rich, intricate tapestry of narratives that span across time and culture. By engaging with the stories of mythical creatures from diverse societies, we've not only traversed geographical boundaries but also temporal ones, discovering how these tales have been woven into the very fabric of human history.

Cultural intersections are at the heart of these myths. They reveal common human concerns and worldviews despite varied cultural backdrops. For example, reflecting on how dragons are depicted in Eastern versus Western mythologies offers insights into societal values and fears, showcasing a profound connection through fantastical tales. This exploration is not just academic; it's a journey into the collective human spirit, uncovering shared dreams and nightmares.

Adaptation and divergence in myths highlight the dynamic nature of cultural narratives. Myths are not static; they evolve as they are told and retold, influenced by the tides of history, migration, and interaction.

Analyzing these changes teaches us about resilience and creativity in human storytelling. It's inspiring to see how cultures adopt elements from each other, adapting them to fit their own unique contexts and needs.

Finally, understanding the ***role of myths in cultural exchange*** has been enlightening. Myths often serve as a medium for cultural dialogue, offering a glimpse into how societies view themselves and others. They can act as bridges or barriers, sometimes reinforcing stereotypes but often encouraging empathy and understanding.

As we reflect on these points, it becomes clear that myths are more than just stories. They are a powerful lens through which we can view the past and present, offering lessons that resonate beyond their narrative scopes. They challenge us to consider our perceptions and encourage us to embrace a more interconnected worldview.

Let's carry forward the curiosity and openness we've cultivated here, allowing these ancient yet living stories to enrich our understanding of both the world and ourselves. Each myth, each creature whispers a truth about humanity, urging us to listen closely and learn eagerly. As we continue this exploration in the remaining chapters, let us remain inspired by the vast mosaic of mythology, always finding new ways to connect with the legends that have shaped human civilization.

Chapter 7: Deciphering Symbols: Context Matters

The Mythical Beast Within the Museum's Walls

In the dimly lit corridors of the museum, Malcolm wandered through the ancient artifacts and sculpted figures of mythical beasts that had once been revered and feared. His shoes echoed softly on the polished stone floor, a rhythmic tapping that seemed to speak with the whispers of history. A curator by profession, he sought stories by passion, especially those woven around creatures that defied explanation yet held deep symbolic meanings across different cultures.

Today, his attention was captured by a new exhibit—an imposing statue of a Griffin from medieval Europe. With its eagle's head and lion's body, the creature symbolized divine power and a guardian of treasures. Malcolm's eyes traced the intricate carvings, noting how the light played off the sharp beak and muscular haunches. It was more than just an artistic marvel; it was a bridge to understanding how people of that era viewed the divine intersection between heaven and earth.

As he stood there, immersed in thought, a group of school children bustled into the room with their teacher. They gathered around him, their young eyes wide with curiosity. *"What does it mean?"* one child asked pointedly, tugging at Malcolm's sleeve.

"It means many things," Malcolm replied, his voice echoing slightly under the high vaulted ceilings. *"To some, it was a protector; to others, a symbol of justice and strength."* He explained how interpretations could shift dramatically depending on cultural contexts and historical moments—how each society painted its fears and aspirations onto these mythical canvases.

The children listened intently as Malcolm spoke about other mythical creatures displayed around them—each story peeling back layers of human fears, desires, and wisdom passed through generations. As they moved from one exhibit to another—the dragon from Eastern mythology, the Sphinx from Egyptian lore—he felt their fascination grow.

It wasn't just about conveying information but connecting these ancient myths to contemporary life. How do we understand our own myths? What beasts do we create from our modern fears and hopes? These questions lingered in his mind as he watched the children depart with bright eyes filled with wonder.

As Malcolm returned to his office tucked away behind the exhibit halls—surrounded by books brimming with folklore and myth—he pondered these connections between past and present. His desk faced a small window where light filtered through in soft beams—perhaps a reminder that understanding is not just found in direct sunlight but also in shadowy nuances.

How might our current symbols be interpreted thousands of years from now?

Unveiling the Truth Behind Mythical Beasts

When we peel back the layers of time and culture surrounding mythical beasts, we uncover not just creatures of fantasy but symbols deeply embedded in the human psyche. To truly understand the significance of these legendary creatures, we must dive into the waters of the cultures and epochs that birthed them.

This exploration is not merely an academic exercise but a journey into the heart of human belief and imagination.

The Crucial Role of Context in Mythical Symbolism

The interpretation of mythical beasts often hinges on the context in which they were conceived. One must understand the historical and cultural backdrop to see a dragon merely as a fearsome beast guarding treasures. However, in Chinese culture, this creature symbolizes power, strength, and good luck—elements that are pivotal to appreciating its role in myths and art. Recognizing this context enriches our understanding and connects us more deeply with those who lived amidst these myths.

Insights Through Historical Lenses

By applying our knowledge of history and culture, we can unveil layers of meaning that remain hidden from the casual observer. Consider the Sphinx's riddle in Greek mythology; it is not just a story element but a reflection of ancient Greek values and challenges. This deeper understanding transforms our view of myths from simple tales to rich narratives shaped by real human experiences and struggles.

Specific Beasts, Specific Meanings

In discussing various mythical creatures—from Norse legends' Fenrir to the Egyptian god Anubis—we will explore how each being served specific symbolic functions within their respective cultures. These stories were not random; they were tailored to communicate themes essential to society's moral fabric and cosmological understanding at that time.

Understanding these symbolic nuances allows us to see beyond the surface and appreciate mythical beasts as complex symbols rather than mere characters in old stories. Our exploration will bridge centuries and continents, bringing us face-to-face with ancient peoples' fears, hopes, and values.

Through this journey into mythological symbolism, *we learn about past civilizations* and reflect on our beliefs and values. By connecting with these ancient symbols, we tap into universal themes that are still relevant today—themes of heroism, morality, and the eternal struggle between good and evil.

As we traverse this chapter, let's keep our minds open to what these legendary creatures can teach us about humanity's past—and perhaps ourselves. The venture is set to be as enlightening as it is enchanting.

Understanding the Need for Context in Mythical Symbolism

Mythical creatures often hold a mirror to the society from which they emerge, reflecting their values, fears, and aspirations. By grasping the cultural and historical context, the true essence of these symbols can be understood and noticed. Just as a tree cannot be fully understood without its roots, mythical symbols cannot be truly appreciated without a deep dive into their origins.

Imagine trying to understand a complex, multifaceted novel by reading only its last chapter. The characters' motivations, the nuances of the plot, and the climax all lose their significance when stripped of the buildup. Similarly, interpreting mythical beasts without their cultural backstory is like looking at only the surface of a vast ocean.

In many cultures, dragons are seen as menacing and destructive.

Yet, in Chinese mythology, they are revered as symbols of power, strength, and good luck. This stark contrast can only be understood through the lens of historical and cultural context, which paints a broader picture of how these creatures are perceived and why.

Another popular mythological figure, the phoenix, illustrates transformation and renewal in Western cultures. However, its symbolism can vary significantly across different cultures, influenced by local myths, religious beliefs, and historical events.

Each interpretation offers unique insights into the collective psyche and values of the society from which it originates.

Understanding the cultural and historical context is essential to genuinely appreciate mythical symbols.

Applying Contextual Knowledge to Mythical Creatures

By delving into the historical backdrop of a mythological creature, we can uncover layers of meaning that take time to be apparent.

The story of the Minotaur, for instance, is not just about a monster in a labyrinth; it reflects the ancient Minoans' complex society, religious rituals, and the human psyche's dark recesses.

Consider the Sphinx, with its human head and lion's body; in ancient Egypt, it symbolized royal power and the sun god's guardian. With this contextual knowledge, one might see a mythical creature, missing the deeper symbolism linked to sovereignty and divine protection.

Exploring these creatures with an understanding of their origins allows us to see them as figments of imagination and vital expressions of human belief and experience. This approach can transform our perception from viewing them as simple story elements to recognizing them as profound symbols loaded with historical significance.

Reflecting on the cultural significance of these symbols can also offer insights into our modern values and how they have been shaped by historical narratives. This reflective approach enriches our understanding of myths and connects us more deeply with our cultural roots.

How might this deeper understanding of mythological symbols influence our perception of history and culture?

Studying Specific Creatures in Their Cultural Settings

The Japanese kitsune, or fox spirit, is fascinating to study within its cultural context. Traditionally seen as a cunning shape-shifter with either benevolent or malevolent intentions, the kitsune's role in folklore can tell us much about the values of honor, loyalty, and the supernatural in Japanese culture.

Similarly, Norse mythology's Jörmungandr, the Midgard Serpent that encircles the earth, speaks volumes about the Norse perception of the world—a harsh, unforgiving, yet interconnected universe.

Each mythical creature, when studied in its original cultural setting, unravels part of the human condition and societal norms of the time.

By examining these creatures through the lens of their cultural and historical contexts, we gain a more comprehensive understanding of not just the myths themselves but also the people who created them. This study illuminates the ways in which myths serve as a bridge between the past and present, continually influencing modern culture and thought.

Exploring these mythical creatures within their original contexts reveals their significance and the timeless human truths they embody, linking cultural knowledge, historical context, and the interpretation of mythical symbolism.

Unveiling the Veil: A Journey Through Mythical Contexts

By exploring myths and their beasts, we've seen just how essential context is to full understanding. The ***cultural and historical backdrops*** from which these myths emerge are not just scenery; they are integral to grasping the profound meanings these stories hold for their tellers and their audiences. Our journey doesn't end here, however. To continue deepening our comprehension, we must actively engage with this context in a structured, thoughtful way.

Step 1: Examine the need for cultural and historical context

Begin by recognizing that every myth is a reflection of the environment that created it. The dragon might symbolize imperial power in one culture or chaos and destruction in another. Consider how the interpretations of creatures like the phoenix could change from one era to another, symbolizing resurrection, renewal, or even fiery destruction based on prevailing cultural sentiments.

Step 2: Apply contextual knowledge to reveal deeper meanings

With this foundation, delve deeper. Take the Sphinx's riddle, for example. Beyond just a challenge to passersby, it embodies the ancient Egyptians' reverence for wisdom and the protection of sacred sites. Reflect on how societal beliefs or historical events shaped these narratives. What does the Sphinx tell us about how those people viewed the unknown or authority?

Step 3: Study specific creatures in their original cultural settings

Choose a creature like the Japanese kitsune, a fox known for its cunning and magical abilities. By understanding Shinto beliefs and the historical significance of the fox in Japanese folklore, one appreciates not just a 'mythical creature' but a pivotal cultural symbol intertwined with notions of spirituality and human morality.

This structured approach—*Unveiling the Veil*—is designed as an academic exercise and a transformational journey. It encourages you to learn about mythical creatures and experience their worlds, understand their origins, and appreciate their lasting impact on contemporary culture. By dedicating time to each step—perhaps a week per stage—you can transform your understanding from surface-level interpretations to profound insights.

Let these stories remind us that myths are more than tales. They are windows into the hearts and minds of our ancestors. Engage with them, reflect on them, and let them enlighten your understanding of the human experience. This is not just learning; it's a journey of discovery.

Chapter 8: Evolving Beasts: A Journey Through Art

How Does Art Capture the Essence of Myth?

In the quiet, sunlit corner of a museum, Thomas stood motionless before a Greek vase painted with scenes of centaurs. The mythic creatures danced around the curve of the ancient pottery, their forms fluid and dynamic. Thomas, an art historian by profession, felt a deep connection to these depictions, understanding them as narratives beyond their visual appeal. Each brushstroke spoke of an era's beliefs and values, encapsulating myths that had morphed over centuries.

The air was still in the room, disturbed only by the soft footsteps of visitors and the gentle murmur of voices discussing art and history.

Thomas shifted his gaze to a nearby Renaissance painting where dragons adorned with intricate scales guarded treasures in landscapes drawn from the artist's imagination. These creatures appeared more menacing than those on the Greek vase—reflecting perhaps a shift in societal fears or fascinations.

As he moved through the gallery, his mind wandered to a modern interpretation he had seen just weeks before—a digital artwork displaying mythical beings in surreal, post-apocalyptic settings.

This stark contrast with classical artworks highlighted technological advancements and contemporary society's anxieties and hopes.

Thomas paused by a window overlooking the garden, where sculptures of nymphs seemed to play among the shadows and sunlight. He pondered how each era's rendition of mythical creatures served as mirrors reflecting human nature: our virtues and vices, dreams and despair.

Does our interpretation of myths change because we change ourselves?

From Chisel to Pixel: Tracing the Artistic Evolution of Mythical Beasts

The way we visualize mythical creatures mirrors the changing tides of human culture and artistic expression. Each brush stroke, chisel mark on the stone, and click in a digital art program tells a story not just of fantastical beings but also of the times and people who created them. This chapter delves into how these depictions have evolved, highlighting how art is a chronicle of our shifting relationship with these legendary beasts.

The Canvas of History

Art is a powerful documentary tool, capturing what societies value, fear, and aspire to. By examining the artistic depictions of mythical creatures through various historical epochs—from the imposing statues of ancient civilizations to the intricate tapestries of the Middle Ages and the dynamic animations of today—we see not only different artistic techniques but also varying interpretations of myth itself. Each era's portrayal tells us about the societal norms, technological advancements, and philosophical ideologies prevalent at that time.

Symbols in Transformation

Mythical creatures often carry heavy symbolic weight. A dragon might represent chaos and danger in one culture or wisdom and protection in another. Tracing how these symbols transform through art over centuries reveals insights into changing cultural attitudes and values. What causes a society to shift its view from fearing to venerating the same creature? This chapter explores these transitions, suggesting that changes in artistic depictions can signal broader shifts in societal norms and beliefs.

Society's Mirror

Moreover, the evolution in depicting mythical beasts often parallels significant societal changes. For instance, during societal upheaval or transformation periods, there might be a noticeable shift towards darker, more menacing representations of mythical creatures.

Conversely, eras focused on exploration and discovery often depict these beings in more curious and majestic ways. This reflection is not merely coincidental but is a profound indicator of the human psyche responding to external environments through creativity.

Artistic interpretations are more than just aesthetic endeavors; they are imbued with layers of cultural significance that can be dissected to reveal deep insights into past and present societies. As we move forward in this chapter, keep an eye on how these visual representations act as both products and influencers of their times.

A Journey Through Artistic Mediums

The materials and methods used to depict mythical creatures also tell a story of technological evolution and artistic experimentation. From ancient stone carvings to sophisticated digital renderings, each medium adds its own texture to the tapestry of mythic representation. This progression is technical and conceptual, influencing how artists conceive and audiences perceive these legendary figures.

Reflecting on Our Own Perceptions

As you engage with this exploration, you might reflect on your perceptions of mythical creatures. Have they been shaped by cultural heritage, personal experiences, or perhaps by the arts themselves? This introspection is vital as it connects us personally to the broader narrative, making history relevant and alive.

By understanding how our ancestors envisioned these creatures through their artistry—and recognizing why they painted, sculpted, or designed them the way they did—we connect with their hopes, fears, and dreams. We also prepare ourselves to continue this legacy—interpreting myths in ways that speak to our contemporary experiences while looking forward to future possibilities.

In embarking on this journey through art's history with mythical beasts, we uncover layers about these enigmatic creatures and about ourselves as viewers and creators within an ever-evolving cultural landscape.

Investigating Artistic Evolution

Art captures more than just beauty; it records history, emotion, and social change. Consider the evolution of mythical creatures in art. In ancient times, these creatures were often depicted with a sense of awe and mystery, carved into the walls of temples or cast in bronze. These early representations highlight a reverence, fear, or worship toward these fantastical beings.

Switching to a metaphorical perspective, imagine if each brushstroke on a canvas or chisel mark on a stone could speak. They would tell tales of societal values and fears, evolving through ages like a tree grows rings. As centuries turned, the artistic depictions of these mythical creatures began to shift, mirroring changes in societal beliefs and technological advancements.

During the Renaissance, for instance, mythical creatures in art began to take on more human-like qualities, reflecting the era's deep dive into humanism. Artists like Leonardo da Vinci and Michelangelo portrayed mythical beings with more emotion and complexity, suggesting a shift in how people related to these myths.

This trend continued into modern times, where mythical creatures have been reimagined in countless forms—from dark and foreboding figures in Gothic art to whimsical and friendly beings in contemporary cartoons and films. Each iteration shows artistic skill and style and encapsulates the prevailing cultural attitudes and technological possibilities of the time.

The key point is that the transformation in artistic depictions of mythical creatures allows us to trace the evolution of societal values and technological advancements over the centuries.

Tracing Symbolism and Significance

Art does not exist in a vacuum. It reflects the beliefs, hopes, and fears of its time. By examining the changing depictions of mythical creatures, one can observe cultural significance and symbolism shifts. Initially, these creatures often served as symbols of the unknown, embodying the fears and mysteries of the natural world.

As societies evolved over time, so too did the symbolic meanings attached to these beings. In medieval art, dragons often represented sin and evil, confronting heroes in battles that symbolized the struggle between good and evil. This portrayal can be seen as a mirror reflecting the intense religiosity of the period.

In contrast, the Enlightenment brought about a reevaluation of these symbols. Mythical creatures like unicorns, once just fantastical beasts, began to symbolize purity and grace, aligning with new values of beauty and goodness. This shift underscores a broader movement towards reason and away from superstition.

Artists play with these symbols, sometimes reinforcing traditional meanings and other times subverting them to offer new interpretations. Consider how contemporary media often uses mythical creatures to explore themes of identity and transformation, significantly different from their traditional roles.

Can observing the evolution of these symbols in art reveal more about our own transformation as a society?

Evaluating Societal Impact

Societies' depictions of mythical creatures in art often reflect their current ideologies, technological capabilities, and cultural climates. For instance, during periods of great societal upheaval or change, such as the Industrial Revolution, depictions of mythical creatures often became darker and more complex, mirroring the anxieties of the time.

Conversely, these creatures might be portrayed in a more light-hearted or benevolent manner in more stable or prosperous times. The opulent art of the Baroque period, with its intricate and embellished depictions of mythical beings, reflects the wealth and grandeur of its time.

The digital age has introduced a new era of mythical depiction.

With tools like CGI, mythical creatures are more lifelike and dynamic than ever, capable of expressing complex emotions and thoughts. This technological advancement allows for a deeper exploration of themes such as ethics and morality.

By studying the artistic evolution of mythical creatures, we gain insights into how societal trends, cultural shifts, and technological advancements have influenced their portrayal.

This understanding enriches our appreciation of art and deepens our comprehension of history and society.

These insights are crucial for anyone keen on understanding the broader context of mythical art and its significance. They serve to connect us more deeply with our past, present, and future, offering a richer tapestry of human experience and imagination.

Throughout this exploration, we've delved deeply into the rich tapestry of how mythical creatures have been portrayed in art across the ages. It's been a journey that showcases artistic talent and reflects profound shifts in societal values and beliefs.

Art as a Mirror of Change: Artistic depictions are more than just visual delights; they reflect societal attitudes and shifts. From the awe-inspiring statues of ancient civilizations to the dynamic digital artworks of today, each piece carries a story—a narrative about the time in which it was created. This visual evolution offers us invaluable insights into how myths have been interpreted and reinterpreted, influenced by the ebb and flow of cultural tides.

Cultural Significance and Symbolism: The symbolism associated with these mythical beings has also transformed dramatically. What once might have been an emblem of fear can evolve to symbolize strength or wisdom. This shift in symbolism is not just an artistic choice but a reflection of changing societal norms and values. By studying these changes, we gain a deeper understanding of the past and present societies—how they have differed and what they have in common.

Impact of Societal Trends: Moreover, the impact of societal trends on these portrayals cannot be overstated. Each era's defining characteristics—Enlightenment, industrialization, or the digital revolution—have influenced how these creatures are depicted. This influence reminds us of how interconnected art and society are; as society changes, so too does its art.

Reflecting on this journey, it becomes clear that the art of mythical creatures is not just about preserving old legends but is a dynamic field that continues to evolve with each passing era. It challenges us to consider how our current representations might be viewed by future generations and what they will reveal about our own time.

I hope this exploration inspires you to look at mythical art as relics of the past and as living dialogues between the old and the new. May it encourage you to discover more, to see beyond the canvas or sculpture, and to find the stories woven into the very fabric of our culture. Let's carry this curiosity and appreciation for art and mythology as we continue our journey through the remaining chapters, uncovering more secrets and stories of legendary beasts.

Chapter 9: Beyond the Myth: Critical Thinking and Synthesis

Can Myths Teach Us More Than Just Stories?

Eleanor sat by the window, the light casting long shadows across the floor, laden with books and papers. Her fingers traced the lines of an ancient Greek text, her mind weaving through the labyrinthine tales of gods and monsters. The air was thick with the scent of old paper and ink, a testament to years spent pursuing understanding.

She paused, her eyes resting on a depiction of an illusion in a medieval manuscript. The creature, a blend of lion, goat, and serpent, seemed to leap from the page in a swirl of impossible anatomy and mythic power. Eleanor's thoughts drifted to her lectures at the university, where discussions often turned spirited when mythology bridged into history. How could she convey that these myths carried more than just fantastical beasts and heroic deeds? They were cultural DNA, encoding values, fears, and aspirations.

The clock ticked audibly in the background as she considered her next class session. She planned to challenge her students to look beyond the surface of these stories and to critically read what was presented and what it represented about ancient societies. Could they see how myths influenced modern perspectives on heroism, justice, or morality? Her mind buzzed with potential discussion points.

A gentle breeze fluttered through the open window, bringing with it the distant sounds of life outside—children's laughter mingled with the cawing of crows. It reminded Eleanor that myths were alive in scholarly texts and breathed life into everyday moments. They shaped laws, inspired art, and even colored political debates without many realizing their origins.

As she gathered her notes for tomorrow's lecture, Eleanor reflected on how each myth held layers of meaning waiting to be uncovered like precious relics within a ruin. Would her students be able to peel back those layers themselves? Could they learn to see not just what myths said about ancient people but what they say about all humanity?

Could understanding these ancient narratives help us navigate our current world complexities?

Unveiling the True Power of Myths

When we delve into the enchanting world of mythical creatures, from the fire-breathing dragons to the elusive unicorns, it's easy to get lost in their awe-inspiring tales. However, this chapter invites you on a journey through these stories and beyond them into a realm where ***critical thinking and synthesis*** guide us. Here, we equip ourselves with the tools to dissect and reconstruct these narratives, enabling a deeper understanding and appreciation of their cultural and historical contexts.

Engaging with Myths on a Deeper Level

Imagine reading about the Greek Hydra, a multi-headed serpent whose heads would regenerate if cut off. A simple reading might leave you thrilled or terrified. Yet, engaging critically with this myth opens up a plethora of questions: What does the Hydra symbolize? How did ancient Greeks interpret this creature? By encouraging such inquiries, we move towards an analytical mindset that seeks stories and understands their underlying messages.

Synthesizing Diverse Perspectives

The beauty of mythology lies not only in its narratives but also in its varied interpretations. Scholars, historians, and artists have depicted mythical creatures in numerous ways over centuries. This chapter will guide you in synthesizing ***these diverse sources***, creating a cohesive understanding that respects historical accuracy and artistic expression. This approach helps bridge gaps between different fields of study, illuminating how interconnected our knowledge is.

Separating Fact from Fiction

One of the most thrilling aspects of studying myths is distinguishing what could be historically plausible from sheer fantastical invention. Was there ever a creature that could be remotely linked to dragons in any real-world biology? Here, we'll explore how to sift through historical evidence and modern representations to discern which elements of these stories are rooted in reality and which are products of creative liberty.

Through this intellectual expedition, you'll find yourself passively consuming myths and actively engaging with them. You'll learn to question, analyze, and synthesize information from various sources, including ancient texts, archaeological findings, and modern reinterpretations by artists and writers.

Why This Matters

Understanding myths through critical thinking doesn't just change how we view old stories; it transforms how we perceive history, culture, and even our current world. It empowers us to recognize patterns in human storytelling. It challenges us to think about why certain themes recur across civilizations.

By the end of this chapter, you will gain deeper insights into legendary beasts and enhance your ability to engage with complex information in any field. This isn't just about mythical mastery; it's about fostering a sharper, more analytical mind that can navigate various forms of knowledge quickly and with insight.

So let us embark on this journey together, armed with curiosity and critical tools, ready to uncover layers of meaning that have waited hidden beneath the surface of captivating tales told since time immemorial.

Developing Critical Reading Skills

Engaging with mythological content requires more than just absorbing stories; it demands a critical eye. Critical reading is the skillful text analysis to uncover deeper meanings and assess its truthfulness. This involves questioning the text, identifying its purposes, and evaluating its sources. For instance, when reading about the legendary Phoenix, ask yourself: What cultural beliefs influenced this myth? Who wrote it, and why?

Imagine you're an archaeologist sifting through layers of soil. Each layer offers artifacts; some are mere fragments, while others are almost intact. Similarly, as a critical reader, you sift through layers of narrative and historical context to find the truth buried within the myth. This process is crucial for separating fact from embellishment.

Another key aspect of critical reading is recognizing biases and perspectives. Authors often write from a specific cultural or personal viewpoint, which can color the portrayal of mythological figures. By identifying these biases, readers can understand the broader context of the myth and appreciate its multifaceted nature.

Critical reading also involves comparing myths with other sources, such as archaeological findings or historical texts. Such cross-referencing can either validate the myth's historical basis or reveal it as a product of its time, shaped by then-prevailing ideologies and knowledge.

Developing strong critical reading skills is essential for a nuanced understanding of mythological content.

Synthesizing Mythological Insights

Synthesis in mythology means integrating information from various narratives and research to form a holistic view. This process starts with gathering diverse perspectives—from ancient scripts to modern interpretations—and then weaving them into a cohesive understanding.

Consider a tapestry depicting a grand battle from a myth. Each thread represents a different narrative or piece of research. Alone, a single thread provides limited insight, but together, they create a detailed and vibrant image. This analogy illustrates the synthesis process: combining multiple sources to fully understand mythological stories.

Engaging in this synthesis involves reading widely and critically analyzing how each piece of information contributes to our understanding of myths. It means looking at how different cultures interpret the same myth and recognizing the underlying themes that transcend cultural boundaries.

The rhetorical question to consider here is How synthesizing various mythological sources help us understand the human condition more deeply?

A Model for Evaluating Mythological Narratives

The SYNTH Framework

The SYNTH Framework—Synthesize, Yield, Navigate, Think, Hypothesize—is a structured approach designed to guide readers through the critical evaluation of mythology. This model encourages deep inquiry and comprehensive understanding.

Synthesize

Begin by synthesizing available information. Gather myths, scholarly articles, and historical data about a mythical figure or event. This initial collection is akin to assembling all the puzzle pieces before attempting to put them together.

Yield

Next, insights from the synthesized data will be yielded by identifying patterns and commonalities. This step is crucial for understanding the core themes of the myth and how they relate to broader human experiences.

Navigate

Navigate through different cultural interpretations of the myth. This involves comparing how various societies have understood and adapted the myth over time. Such comparison enriches your understanding and highlights the cultural dynamics that influence mythological narratives.

Think

Think critically about the implications of the myth. What does it reveal about the society from which it originated? What moral or philosophical questions does it raise? Analyzing these aspects helps grasp the more profound significance of myths beyond their narrative structures.

Hypothesize

Finally, hypothesize about the myth's relevance today. How do the themes and lessons resonate with current societal issues? This reflection helps apply the insights gained from ancient myths to modern-day contexts.

By following the *SYNTH Framework*, readers can systematically break down and explore the complexities of mythological narratives. This model not only aids in distinguishing between historically supported facts and modern interpretations but also enhances the overall appreciation of mythology as a reflection of human culture and psychology.

By mastering critical reading, synthesizing diverse sources, and distinguishing between historical and modern narratives, we can profoundly understand mythology.

The journey through understanding mythology deeply is both enlightening and intricate. Critical reading and synthesis are not merely academic tools but ***essential skills*** that enable us to navigate the vast seas of mythological narratives with discernment and appreciation. Through the careful analysis of texts, whether ancient scriptures or modern interpretations, we hone our ability to see beyond the surface. This skill set is crucial, as it empowers us to piece together various perspectives and create a more rounded understanding of mythical stories.

Reflecting on the process of distinguishing between what is historically supported and what is a product of modern fabrication is akin to being a detective in a world brimming with folklore and legends. The satisfaction of unraveling these stories, to reveal the threads of truth woven into the fabric of mythology, is profoundly rewarding. Each myth, each artifact, and each scholarly article offers a piece of a larger puzzle. When we synthesize these pieces, the resulting image is both beautiful and informative, providing deeper insights into the cultures and times from which these myths originated.

This intellectual engagement with mythology does more than just expand our knowledge. It connects us with the thinkers, artists, and storytellers of the past. It's a form of time travel that allows us to converse with history, understanding the *'what'* and *'how,'* and the *'why'* behind these legendary narratives. Such connections are not only academically enriching but are also personally transformative.

They remind us that we are part of a continuum, learning from those who came before us while contributing our own voices to the ongoing dialogue about human experience and imagination.

Moreover, embracing these skills sets a foundation for more informed discussions about mythology. We become contributors to a larger conversation that values precision and depth. Our discussions then have the power to inspire others, to educate, and perhaps most importantly, to preserve the integrity of these timeless stories for future generations.

Therefore, let us continue approaching mythological studies with curiosity and criticality. Let us be diligent in our reading, thoughtful in our synthesis, and discerning in our conclusions. In doing so, we honor the legacy of myths and enrich our lives with their timeless wisdom and enduring wonder.

Chapter 10: Connecting with the Cosmic Dance: Mythical Creatures and Human Themes

In the Shadows of Mythical Beasts

Ella walked through the dusky streets of her small town, the cobblestones cool and uneven beneath her feet. The air carried a crispness that hinted at the coming winter. Her mind wandered to the lecture she had attended earlier in the day about mythical creatures and their enduring presence in human culture. She thought about dragons, griffins, and other fantastical beasts that symbolized the eternal struggle between chaos and order, good and evil.

As she passed by the old library, its ancient bricks seemed to whisper stories of times long past. She could almost hear the flutter of wings or the distant roar of a mythical beast challenging a daring hero. These tales, she realized, were not just relics of human imagination but mirrors reflecting our deepest fears and highest aspirations.

Inside her cozy living room, with a mug of steaming tea cradled in her hands, Ella pondered how these mythical creatures might help her understand her own life's turmoil. Recently, her community had been divided over plans to develop a historic part of town into a modern shopping center. The debate was fierce, with arguments flaring like dragonfire. Was this not a battle between preserving order and succumbing to chaotic change?

Her neighbor, Mr. Jacobsen, knocked gently on her door, his face lined with concern. He shared his fears about losing his home to make way for new construction. Listening to him, Ella felt a surge of protective energy. These ancient myths could offer wisdom on how to navigate this modern conflict.

As Mr. Jacobsen spoke earnestly about his love for their shared heritage—a theme as timeless as any epic saga—Ella saw parallels in their story with those age-old battles between mortal desires and divine wills depicted in myths. Here was their dragon to slay: unbridled development threatening their community's soul.

Could understanding these universal themes help them preserve what truly mattered? As she bid Mr. Jacobsen goodnight, Ella felt fortified by their connection—a bond as strong as any legendary alliance.

What lessons can we draw from mythical creatures when facing our own community's dragons?

Beyond Myths: Embracing the Dance of Life and Legend

Embarking on this journey through *"Mythical Mastery,"* we've traversed landscapes populated by dragons, danced with unicorns, and soared with griffins. Each creature, a mosaic of cultural heritage and human emotion, has offered us a unique lens to view the world. As we near the end of our exploration, Chapter 10 invites us to delve deeper, connecting these mythical beings to the universal rhythms of human existence. Here, we do not just recount tales of fantasy but weave them into the very fabric of our daily lives.

Mythical creatures serve as mirrors, reflecting our deepest fears, highest aspirations, and ongoing struggles. These narratives are not just relics of ancient civilizations but are vibrant with themes that resonate universally—good versus evil, chaos versus order, mortal versus divine. Understanding these themes allows us to see ourselves in these stories, bridging epochs and cultures through shared human experiences.

In this chapter, we will explore how these enduring themes manifest in mythical narratives and what they reveal about our own lives. By examining the symbolism embedded in these legendary beasts, we can uncover insights into our own worldviews and personal challenges. This is an academic exercise and a journey toward self-discovery and connection.

Reflecting on Good Versus Evil

The battle between good and evil is the most foundational theme in mythology. It informs our understanding of morality, ethics, and justice. We'll explore how different cultures interpret this dichotomy through their mythical beasts and what this tells us about their—and our own—moral compasses.

Symbols for Today

Ancient symbols carry timeless wisdom. By decoding the symbols associated with mythical creatures—such as the dragon's fire or the unicorn's horn—we can apply their lessons to contemporary issues. This section will help you translate these ancient symbols into tools for personal growth and understanding.

Insights into the Human Condition

Finally, we'll examine how mythical creatures offer a window into the human condition across different times and places. What fears did they embody? What hopes did they represent? Understanding this can deepen our empathy for others and ourselves, linking us more closely to humanity's continuous story.

Through *"Mythical Mastery,"* we've equipped ourselves with knowledge of mythical beasts and their significance in art, literature, and cultural discourse. Our final chapter builds on this foundation, guiding you toward a more profound appreciation of how these legends inform and enrich our lives today.

By engaging with mythical creatures in this reflective manner, we're invited to partake in a cosmic dance that is both ancient and perpetually new—a dance where each step teaches us more about who we were, who we are, and perhaps most importantly, who we might become. Let's embrace this dance together, finding in it the rhythm of our own stories woven into the grand tapestry of human history.

Exploring Universal Themes Reflected in Mythical Narratives

Mythical creatures often embody the stark dichotomy of good versus evil, a theme that resonates deeply within human narratives.

Consider the dragons in European folklore, which frequently represent chaos and destruction, usually standing against heroes who symbolize order and goodness. These stories frame the creatures as beasts to be slain and as essential components of a moral lesson about bravery and virtue.

Imagine a vast, dark forest where a dragon lurks, embodying fear and chaos. The hero's journey into this forest can be seen as a metaphor for our battles against our own fears and hardships. Just as the hero confronts the dragon, we confront our challenges, striving to overcome them with courage and integrity.

In many cultures, the representation of good and evil in mythical narratives serves to teach societal values and norms. These stories are crafted not merely for entertainment but to impart crucial societal wisdom that helps maintain social order. Through these tales, listeners learn about the virtues of courage, honesty, and perseverance.

The cyclical battle between good and evil in myths mirrors our ongoing struggles in life. Just like the ever-repeating stories of heroes vanquishing monsters, our lives are full of moments where we must rise to meet various challenges, embodying the heroes of our own stories.

Mythical narratives allow us to reflect on the eternal struggle between good and evil, teaching us about our values and strengths.

Relating Ancient Mythical Symbols to Contemporary Life

The symbols and themes from ancient myths still echo in today's world, offering a bridge between the past and our contemporary experiences. Take, for instance, the myth of Phoenix, which symbolizes renewal and rebirth. This powerful symbol resonates with anyone experiencing a significant change or recovery, emphasizing the possibility of new beginnings and hope.

How often do we see the themes of rebirth and transformation mirrored in our own lives? Whether it's recovering from a loss or making a significant life change, the Phoenix reminds us that we can rise from the ashes of our circumstances, renewed and strong.

Mythical symbols also serve as a cultural shorthand, carrying complex ideas across generations in an accessible format. These symbols are not static; they evolve with our societies, adapting to new values and contexts while retaining their core significance.

Consider how the narrative of a battle against giants might be seen in personal struggles against seemingly insurmountable challenges.

The giants in our lives could be personal fears, societal pressures, or even physical obstacles.

Could your own life experiences be viewed through the lens of these ancient symbols, providing context and empowerment?

Appreciating Insights into the Human Condition Through Mythical Creatures

Mythical creatures often serve as mirrors reflecting the multifaceted aspects of the human condition. They embody our fears, aspirations, conflicts, and virtues across various cultures and epochs. The Hydra, a multi-headed serpent from Greek mythology, represents the idea that life's problems can often multiply if tackled incorrectly.

This insight into human nature is timeless. Some challenges require more than brute force; they need strategic thinking and perseverance. Isn't it often that another arises when we solve one problem, much like cutting off one of Hydra's heads, only for more to grow?

By studying these mythical creatures, we gain insights not only into ancient human thought but also into universal psychological truths that are applicable today. These creatures teach us about resilience, adaptability, and the complexity of human and societal challenges.

In a way, mythical creatures are like old friends who know humanity's deep secrets. They bring those secrets into our contemporary world, helping us understand more about ourselves and our societies.

Mythical creatures bridge the divide between ancient wisdom and modern life, offering timeless insights into the human experience.

Their stories are more than just tales; they are reflections of our deepest struggles, hopes, and transformations.

Throughout this journey, we have unraveled the intricate tapestry of myths that bind humanity across different eras and cultures. By delving into the depths of legendary creatures, from dragons to unicorns, we have encountered stories of awe and mystery and unlocked profound insights into the human spirit.

As we've explored, mythical creatures are not mere products of fantasy but reflections of our deepest fears, hopes, and moral struggles. The battles between good and evil, chaos juxtaposed with order, and the mortal in dialogue with the divine are universal themes that resonate within each of us. These narratives encourage us to reflect on our own lives and the values we hold dear, making ancient myths relevant even in modern times.

This chapter shows how these legendary beings help us connect with these universal themes, offering a bridge between the past and present. They serve as mirrors reflecting our collective human experiences and individual journeys. By understanding their symbolic meanings, we enrich our knowledge of history and culture and gain insights into our own lives.

Reflecting on our personal experiences through mythology's lens can be enlightening and transformative. It empowers us to perceive our challenges and triumphs through a broader, more interconnected perspective. This process deepens our self-awareness and enhances our empathy towards others, recognizing that the themes played out in mythical narratives are also woven into the fabric of our daily lives.

As we close this chapter and this book, let us carry forward the wisdom gleaned from these mythical realms. Let these creatures inspire us to live more richly and see the world through a lens of wonder and interconnectedness. The stories of mythical beasts are not just tales from the past; they are ever-present guides that encourage us to face life's complexities with courage and integrity.

Let's continue to explore, learn, and grow, inspired by the legends of old yet anchored in the realities of our world today. May the journey through mythology continue to be one of discovery and inspiration, reminding us that we are all part of a larger, more magical story.

Epilogue

The Enchanted Conclusion: Weaving Wisdom from Myths into Modern Life

As we draw the curtains on our exploration of legendary beasts, it's important to reflect on the intertwining paths of myth and modernity. Our journey through ancient tales and mystical creatures has not just been about quenching curiosity—it's been about understanding the deep-seated symbols that shape our worldviews, art, and philosophies.

Mythical creatures, from dragons to unicorns, have more than just entertainment value; they serve as archetypes reflecting human fears, aspirations, and morals. By delving into their stories, we unlock layers of cultural wisdom that can enrich our personal and professional lives. For artists, these creatures provide endless inspiration for creativity. For educators and students, they serve as tools to engage with cultural heritage in a more profound way.

We've traveled through dense forests of folklore to unearth these beings' origins, understand their narrative arcs, and understand their evolution across cultures. This book aims to make you feel like an explorer, piecing together fragments of ancient knowledge to reveal the cultural significance that mythical beasts hold in our collective psyche.

To truly benefit from this newfound knowledge, I encourage you to incorporate these symbols into your creative endeavors—be it writing, art, or dialogue. Discuss these beings in classrooms, workshops, or casual conversations to keep the rich tapestry of mythology alive.

It's also vital to acknowledge that while we've covered extensive ground, the realm of mythology is vast and varied. There remain many untold stories and interpretations ripe for exploration. I invite you to continue researching and sharing your insights on mythical beings perhaps not covered in this book or to revisit those that have captivated your imagination the most.

Let this book be a springboard into a larger pool of discovery.

Take action by joining online forums, attending seminars on mythology, or starting a creative project inspired by one of the legendary beasts we've discussed. Let the myths you love inform your views and creations.

In closing, remember that myths are not just relics of the past; they are living narratives that continue to shape our future. They remind us of where we've come from and inspire us about where we can go. Carry forward the torch of storytelling—one of the most potent ways to ignite the human spirit.

"Myths are public dreams, dreams are private myths." – Joseph Campbell.

This quote beautifully encapsulates our journey through *"Mythical Mastery."* As you turn each page and uncover each myth, you weave a part of these public dreams into your private tapestry of understanding and imagination. May your path be ever enriched with the magic of old tales and new understandings.

Don't miss out!

Visit the website below and you can sign up to receive emails whenever Myrddin Sage publishes a new book. There's no charge and no obligation.

https://books2read.com/r/B-A-JBAOB-ZVALF

BOOKS 2 READ

Connecting independent readers to independent writers.

Also by Myrddin Sage

Echoes of the Ancient: Unlocking the Mysteries of Celtic Myth
Mythic Japan: Unlocking the Legends of Gods and Heroes
Echoes of Enchantment: Navigating the Magic of Celtic Mythology
Warriors and Wizards: The Heroes of Celtic Myth
Echoes of Valhalla: Unveiling the Modern Wisdom of Norse Myths
Gods Among Us: The Power and Intrigue of Roman Mythology
The Sword and the Sage: Unveiling the Truth of Excalibur and Merlin
Myth Unleashed: Rediscovering the Legends of Hercules and the Pantheon
Echoes of the Gods: Rediscovering the Heroes and Deities of Ancient Egypt
Ancient Echoes: Embracing Egyptian Wisdom in Our Modern World
Alexander the Great Uncovered: A Journey Beyond the Battlefield
Ghost Buster's Guide: The Truth Behind Paranormal Claims
The Grand Mage Wars: The Battle of Legends Unfold
The Grand Mage Wars: The Battle of Legends Unfold
Mythical Mastery: Uncovering the Secrets of Legendary Beasts

About the Author

At 67, Myrddin Sage steps into the spotlight as a newly published author, bringing a tapestry of rich life experiences and a vibrant imagination. His journey from a Navy Veteran to a Retired Dispatcher of Messengers has endowed him with profound insights into human cultures and the natural world. As Myrddin introduces his debut novel, he shares a narrative infused with wisdom, whimsy, and a deep respect for the interconnectedness of life. Drawing on his academic background and extensive travels, Myrddin's work explores themes of adventure, discovery, and the transformative power of knowledge. With his first publication, he proves that new chapters can be embarked upon at any stage of life, inspiring readers with the message that it is always the right time to follow one's passions.

www.ingramcontent.com/pod-product-compliance
Lightning Source LLC
LaVergne TN
LVHW040949150826
845672LV00002B/610

* 9 7 9 8 2 3 0 9 5 1 6 8 1 *